THE BUDDHIST SANGHA

Paradigm of the Ideal Human Society

The Reverend Sunanda Putuwar
(MA., M.T.S., Ph.D.)

UNIVERSITY
PRESS OF
AMERICA

Lanham • New York • London

Copyright © 1991 by Sunanda Putuwar
University Press of America®, Inc.
4720 Boston Way
Lanham, Maryland 20706

3 Henrietta Street
London WC2E 8LU England

Library of Congress Cataloging-in-Publication Data

Putuwar, Sunanda, Rev., 1946-
The Buddhist Sangha : paradigm of the ideal human society
/ by Reverend Sunanda Putuwar.
p.   cm.
Includes bibliographical references and index.
1. Monasticism and religious orders, Buddhist.   I. Title.
BQ6082.P88   1991   294.3'657—dc20   91-14120 CIP

ISBN 0–8191–8279–6 (cloth ed. : alk. paper)
ISBN 0–8191–7842–X (pbk. : alk. paper)

 The paper used in this publication meets the minimum requirements of
American National Standard for Information Sciences—Permanence
of Paper for Printed Library Materials, ANSI Z39.48–1984.

DEDICATED TO

My beloved parents, Mr. Kajibahadura and Mrs.
Dirghamaya Putuwar
"Brahmá ti mátápitaro" (parents are
the most supreme God, Brahmá) ___ The Buddha,
The Anguttara-Nikáya. II. 70.

iii

ACKNOWLEDGEMENTS

This dissertation, except for the section entitled, Exploring Celibacy in the Buddhist Sangha which has been added to it later, was submitted to the Department of Philosophy and Religion at The American University in Washington, D.C., as a partial fulfillment of the requirements for my Ph.D. degree in Philosophy granted on May 15, 1988. My sincere thanks go to Professor Charles S.J. White, Chairman of my Ph.D. Committee, for kindly giving me a helping hand, straightforward advice and welcome, useful comments on my dissertation, to Professor Roger Simonds, the Chairman of the Department of Philosophy and Religion, for his wise assistance, and to Professor George Zachariah in the Department of Philosophy at the University of the District of Columbia, for reading my dissertation.

I must express profound appreciation to The American University for granting me scholarships and graduate assistantships for this study and to the Reverend Thanh Dam, the President of the Buddhist Congregational Church of America in Washinton, D.C. for kindly supporting me during my studies. My sincere thanks go to the Washington Buddhist Vihára also for allowing me to use its library.

And last but not least, my sincere thanks go to Mr. Robert (Bobby) W. Johnson and Professor Robin Schwarz for proofreading my English.

TABLE OF CONTENTS

CHAPTER I

HISTORICAL BACKGROUND

Introduction

The main focus of this research is to analyze the ethical aspects of early Páli (Theraváda) Buddhism. It is a comprehensive, philosophical, systematic, and critical examination of Buddhist ethics and related political principles, whose purpose is to show the Buddhist Sangha as a paradigm of the ideal society.

The theme of political ideas in the original Buddhist texts and commentaries has been ignored both by those who traditionally disdain such an investigation and by modern scholars who dismiss it (See APPENDIX for the detailed source of information). This work will directly address the Sangha politics which have been scorned for so long and exhibit the Sangha as a beau ideal for the society. Such an investigation will show a core of ethical ideas and a political ideal which are applicable to the modern age. These ideas are not connected with a particular political group; rather, they are of a general political nature rarely found within the precepts of most religions.

The Buddha placed great emphasis on non-violence (ahiṁsá); therefore, people hold Buddhism to be a peaceful religion and use it as an implementation for social development as well as an imperative for political peace. The Buddha advocated khanti, which means forbearance, patience, forgiveness, and utthánasampadá (progress) in society. It is known how successful he was in his advocacy of peace; therefore, he must have had a strategy which could contribute greatly to the value system in a complex modern society. The way the Buddha viewed social problems and the means by which he solved these dilemmas are the basis of this strategy. His solutions to these problems contribute to the value of Buddhist philosophy and freedom of thought and speech is the essential element of democracy in this Buddhist political system. Thus, we understand the concept of "democracy" as a system in which everyone is treated equally [i.e., under good law (dhamma) all people are equal.]

From the study of the earliest teachings in the Vinaya-Piṭaka, one can safely say that evidently the Buddha did not explicitly create any rules in the early period

1

of the religion. He taught only principles, or good laws (dhamma) necessary for the attainment of nibbána. The dhammas, for example, are the four noble truths (catu ariya saccam),[1] the noble eightfold path (ariyo atthangikomaggo),[2] the three characteristics of phenomena (ti lakkhana dhamma),[3] the application of mindfulness (satipatthána),[4] and the seven constituents of Enlightenment (satta bojjhanga).[5] In the early period people went to the Buddha genuinely seeking his spiritual guidance to a noble path (ariyamagga). Examples of this approach can be found in the case of pancavaggiya bhikkhus (a group of five ascetics), and the case of Yasa and his friends (Vimala, Subáhu, Punnaji, and Gavampati). All of these individuals heard the teachings, attained enlightenment and were gradually ordained as monks by the Buddha with a simple formula, "Ehi bhikkhu... upasampadá," or, "come, O monks..." Before the existence of the Sangha, the Buddha ordained monks in this way. At the very first ordination, the Buddha did not require anything from his candidates. Over time, a large number of people sought his teachings and some culminated their efforts by being ordained as monks.

---

[1]The four noble truths are: suffering (dukkha), cause of suffering (dukkha samudaya), cessation of suffering (dukkha nirodha), and the way leading to the cessation of suffering (dukkha nirodha gámini patipadá).

[2]The noble eightfold path is: right view (sammá ditthi, right intention or thought (sammá sankappo), right speech (sammá vácá), right conduct (sammá kammanto), right livelihood (sammá ájívo), right effort (sammá váyámo), right mindfulness (sammá sati), and right concentration (sammá samádhi).

[3]The three characteristics are: impermanence (aniccam), and flux or suffering (dukkham), non-soul (anattá).

[4]Contemplation of the body (káyánupassaná), contemplation of feelings (vedanánupassaná), contemplation of mind (cittánupassaná), and contemplation of mental objects (dhammánupassaná).

[5]These are: Mindfulness (sati), investigation of the truth (dhammavicaya), energy (viriya), joy (píti), serenity (passaddhi), meditation rapture (samádhi), and equanimity (upekkhá).

They practiced the <u>dhamma</u> sincerely and achieved attainment commensurate with their practice-levels even without being taught the <u>vinaya</u>-rules.

Eventually, the Buddha began spreading good laws (<u>dhamma</u>) and disciplinary rules (<u>vinaya</u>). He said that "<u>apárutá tessam amatassa dvárá ye sotavanto, pamuñcantu saddhaṁ</u>."[6] In addition, he wanted to make sure that his disciples carried on the same teachings once he revealed them to the world. He wanted to see that mankind was properly organized. He also wanted society to run prosperously and smoothly without any deviation from moral precepts. Furthermore, he desired that mankind attain the ultimate goal, <u>nibbána</u>, in life. When the Sangha had grown to the number of sixty-one members (including the Buddha himself), he qualified all those monks as missionaries and sent them in different directions to spread his message. Before their departure, he urged them in his farewell blessing:

> <u>caratha bhikkhave cárikaṁ bahujanahitáya</u>
> <u>bahujanasukháya lokánukampáya attháya hitáya</u>
> <u>sukháya devamanussánaṁ.   má ekena dve</u>
> <u>agamittha.   desetha bhikkhave dhammaṁ</u>
> <u>ádikalyánaṁ majjhekalyánaṁ pariyosánakalyánaṁ</u>
> <u>sátthaṁ savyañjanaṁ kevalaparipunnaṁ</u>
> <u>parisuddhaṁ brahmacariyaṁ pakásetha.</u>[7]

---

[6]"Open for those who have ears are the doors of immortality (the noble path). Let them give up their wrong faith (<u>saddhá</u>)." Hermann Oldenberg, ed., <u>The Vinaya Piṭakam (The Mahávagga)</u>, Vol. I (London: Published for the Páli Text Society by Luzac & Company, LTD., 1964), p. 7.

[7]"Go monks, travelling for the benevolence and blessings of many, for the happiness and welfare of many, out of compassion for the world, for Gods and humans; teach the <u>dhamma</u> which is lovely at the beginning (<u>ádikalyánaṁ</u>), lovely in the middle (<u>majjhekalyánaṁ</u>) and lovely at the end (<u>pariyosánakalyánaṁ</u>). Do not go two of you on the same way (this was important because the number of monks was supposedly small and therefore they had to spare themselves in order to go to as many places as possible for this noble purpose)." Hermann Oldenberg, ed., <u>The Vinaya Piṭakaṁ (The Mahávagga)</u>, Vol. I (London: Published for the Páli Text Society by Luzac & Company, LTD., 1964), p. 21.

These instructions are evidence of his having formulated at least some formal rules. The Buddha told the monks that he would also go to Uruvela (an area in Northern India) in order to teach <u>dhamma</u>. However, according to Buddhaghosa's Commentary, monks were cautioned to, "let not two persons adopt the same procedure." In their travels, one monk taught while the other kept silent.[8] Buddhaghosa's version came to be accepted by Buddhist scholars.

It is very interesting for us to consider how the society acted towards the missionaries of the Buddha. Evidently this mission affected the entire society because it brought on a cultural revolution. Everywhere in what is now called the modern Indian subcontinent (<u>jambudïpa</u>), there was the sound of praise for the Buddha, the Dhamma, and the Sangha. It has been recorded that the Buddha was praised for his noble body of right conduct, his self-concentration and his intelligence.[9] The Buddha was master of humanity and divinity (<u>satthádevamanussánaṁ</u>), his teachings were good for all and his Sangha members were expected to be virtuous, content and kind to the public.

Some people were jealous of the Buddha. They played cruel tricks against him.[10] They verbally abused,[11] and disputed his doctrinal campaign.[12] Some

---

[8]<u>The Book of the Kindred Sayings (Samyutta-Nikáya)</u>, Part I, translated by Rhys Davids (London: Published for The Páli Text Society by Luzac & Company, LTD., 1950), p. 132.

[9]<u>Dialogues of the Buddha</u>, Part I, translated by T.W. Rhys Davids (London: Published by the Páli Text Society, 1973), p. 245; p. 268.

[10]H.C. Norman, ed., <u>The Commentary of the Dhammapada</u>, Vol. I (London: Published for the Páli Text Society by Luzac & Company, LTD., 1970) pp. 211-212.

[11]<u>Dialogues of the Buddha</u>, Part I, translated by T.W. Rhys Davids, p. 1; Ibid., p. 245; p. 268.

[12]<u>The Middle Length Sayings (Majjhima-Nikáya)</u>, Vol. II, translated by I.B. Horner (London: Published for the Páli Text Society by Luzac & Company, LTD., 1970), p. 39 ff.

even attempted to bribe[13] the head of state, King Pasenadi of Kosala, in order that he oppose the Buddha. However, their efforts were not successful. The Buddha taught his monks not to bear malice when outsiders spoke against him, the Dhamma or the Sangha, nor to be too proud or uplifted when outsiders praised them. In either case, they were to listen attentively and give an explanation (reason) of these things whether they were praised or criticized. The monks were to explain what was true and acceptable and what was not. Otherwise, the monks themselves would be removed from the goal of self-conquest.[14]

The attitude of the Sangha, with an aloof and detached view of the world, impressed the majority of the general public. The high officials and kings supported the Buddha[15] and his missionaries.

According to Theravàda tradition, the Commentary of Dhàtuvibhanga Sutta informs us that King Bimbisàra of Magadha himself, took part in spreading Buddhism. He inscribed on a golden plate, four cubits long and a span in breadth, a description of the Triple Gem: the Buddha, the Dhamma and the Sangha. The various tenets of the Lord Buddha, for instance, the four settings of mindfulness (satipaṭṭhàna), the noble eightfold path, and the thirty-seven constituent factors of Enlightenment appeared on the plate. King Bimbisàra took it to the frontier of his kingdom for another ruler King Pukkusàti.[16] Thus, within a decade the influence of the Buddha even reached kings very effectively.

Pukkusàti, on learning about what was written on this plate, became extremely happy. He shaved off his hair and donned the saffron robes of a monk.

---

[13]V. Fausboll, The Jàtaka Together with its Commentary Being Tales of the Anterior Births of Gotama Buddha, Vol. II (London: Published for the Pàli Text Society by Luzac & Company, LTD., 1963), p. 169 ff.

[14]Dialogues of the Buddha, Part I, p. 3.

[15]See H.C. Norman, ed., The Commentary on the Dhammapada, Vol. I, p. 218.

[16]G.P. Malalasekera, Dictionary of Pàli Proper Names, Vol. II (London: Published for the Pàli Text Society by Luzac & Company, LTD., 1960), p. 215.

He sought out the Buddha and heard the Dhátuvibhanga Sutta[17] preached. These two neighboring kings had great affection for each other. From the activities and devotion of King Bimbisára, one can see that he voluntarily tried his best to promote the teachings of the Buddha (Buddhasásana), showing that there must have been some political validity in them.

The Buddha's primary mission encompassed not only human beings but non-human beings (amanussa) as well. His ethical teachings and prudent counselling automatically reached, directly or indirectly, political campaigns and cultural revolutions on a local and national level. Hence, we accept the rationality of the ethical ideal which says that when the citizens are good and act ethically, the country itself is good. A country does not become good or bad, developed or under-developed apart from the practices of its citizens. The professions and behaviors of people show the country's character.

The mission of spiritual help to individual devotees and societal groups reached near and far. It helped scholars recognize the Buddha's teachings as beneficial to the country and as an aid to peace. For this reason, it can be said that the Buddha's mission caused political campaigns for peace and a type of social management to develop. More importantly, he helped enrich the culture of India at this time. From this, one can understand how a moral lesson can become part of political ideas. Kings of the countries of the Indian subcontinent were impressed with and influenced by the political and organizational structure of the Sangha.[18]

---

[17]Ibid.; The Middle Length Sayings (Majjhima-Nikáya), Vol. III, translated from the Pali by I.B. Horner (London: Published for the Páli Text Society by Luzac & Company, LTD., 1959), p. 285 ff.

[18]Once the Buddha was staying in Mango Grove in Rajagaha with a company of twelve hundred and fifty monks. One moonlit night, Jïvaka led King Ajátasattu and his large entourage to this same grove. The King was mentally tormented because he had committed the grave sin of killing his righteous father for power. The King visited the Buddha in search of mental peace. When he came to the perfectly quiet Mango Grove, the king was seized with a sudden fear and consternation. The hairs on his body stood erect. He thought that his father's physician, Jïvaka, might have deceived him with a conspiracy to betray him to his foes. "How can it be so quiet -- no sound at all, not a sneeze nor a cough, in so large an assembly of brethren," he wondered? However, Jïvaka was able to

According to Buddhist accounts, the largest congregation of followers that the Buddha converted at one setting was twelve million (nahuta) brahmans and householders led by King Bimbisára.[19] In this way, his teachings had an affect on the entire social and political condition of Jambudïpa (what is now equivalent to Nepal, and the modern Indian subcontinent).

The result of the Buddha's efforts was a rapid increase in the Sangha population. This necessitated the creation of various disciplinary rules and the formation of constitutional laws. These laws, which constitute the Vinaya-Pitaka reached 227 in number and were established with the help of the Sangha members.

A common theme in the Vinaya is the relationship of the Sangha to the laity. King Bimbisára was instrumental in helping to establish some of the formal codes for monks. The Pátimokkha (the summary of the moral codes) formalized relations between the Sangha and the laity. The first example of this formalized relationship is obvious in that the monks regularly gave instruction on dhamma. The king, who observed and evaluated the social activities in his country, noticed that wanderers (ájïvakas) of other religious sects gathered together on the fourteenth (cátuddasï), fifteenth (pannarasi) and eighth/sabbath (atthami/uposatha) days of the half month (pakkha). People gathered to discuss and listen to dhamma talks. In this way, people gained affection and respect for other religious wanderers and even gained faith and became followers. This social religious interaction was mutually beneficial for the wanderers as well as the laity.

---

convince him that he played no trick. There was no betrayal whatsoever. After proceeding ahead with Jïvaka's persuasion, King Ajátasattu saw the perfectly calm and quiet assembly of monks! He was so surprised and impressed. As he respectfully "stood and looked on the assembly, seated in perfect silence, calm as a clear lake, he broke out: "Would that my son, Udáyi Bhadda, might have such calm as this assembly of brethren now has!": Dialogues of the Buddha, Part I, translated from the Páli by T.W. Rhys Davids (London: Published by the Páli Text Society, 1973), pp. 67-68. No wonder he was greatly impressed by this display. He sent his thoughts to his beloved son. Would not it be hard even for a king with his mandatory laws and arms to keep such a large assembly perfectly calm and quiet? The Buddha controlled his Sangha even without a stick or weapon.

[19]The Mahávagga translated by I.B. Horner, p. 28.

King Bimbisára was favorably impressed by those gatherings on Observance days and was anxious to experience the same thing within the Buddhist Sangha.

One day King Bimbisára approached the Buddha to see if it was all right to set up the same kind of religious- social interactions. The Buddha consented to the request. In fact, he rejoiced in the idea of King Bimbisára and delighted him with talk about the dhamma. Later on, in this same vein, the Buddha addressed the monks and allowed them to assemble on the fourteenth and fifteenth days of the half month[20] to speak about dhamma. This is how the formal interaction between the Sangha and laity came into being.

Having established the Sangha and the community of lay disciples, the duties and responsibilities of both parties were clearly perceived and reciprocated. From these events the Buddhist Sangha developed an entire religious and educational institution. The religious gathering gave birth to social and political ideas and systems. On the same basis of these gatherings, the Buddha eventually advised the Sangha to recite the Patimokkha, the key doctrine for monastic institutional life. This recitation ensures the harmonious unity of the Sangha itself. During this ceremony monks have the opportunity to see each other. They may exchange friendly greetings and make individual confessions or they may admonish one another about the good laws (dhamma) and disciplinary rules and regulations (vinaya). A clear description of this is presented in the section on The Disciplinary Rules and Regulations.

The Buddha did not want to pass away into parinibbána until there were capably trained monks, nuns, and male and female lay disciples who would confidently carry on the sublime dhamma. When Mára, the Evil One, asked him to die, the Buddha responded,

> na táváham pápima parinibbáyissámi, yáva
> me bhikkhú na sávaka bhávissanti viyattá vinïtá
> visáradá pattayogakkhemá bahussutá dhammadhará
> dhammánudhammappatipanná sámïcippatipanná
> anudhammacárino sakam ácariyakam uggahetvá
> ácikkhissanti desessanti paññápessanti

---

[20]Ibid., pp. 130-131.

paṭṭhapessanti vivarissanti vibhajissanti uttānīkarissanti, uppannaṁ parappavādaṁ sahadhammena suniggahitaṁ niggahetvā sappāṭihāriyaṁ dhammaṁ desessantī'ti.[21]

After having done 45 years of service to humanity and _devas_ (Gods), the Buddha passed away. A monk named Subhadda was relieved by the death of the Buddha. He told the lamenting monks that it was better to be rid of the Master's presence so that monks would have freedom to do as they wished, and no longer be bound by his laws.[22] Subhadda's view threatened to cause the dissolution of the teachings (_sāsana_) and the Sangha. Therefore, Venerable Mahá Kassapa opposed Subhadda's view and proposed that five hundred of the most eminent monks gather at Rajagaha in order to compile the Buddha's teachings into an authentic text.[23] This helped preserve the good laws (_dhamma_), and the disciplinary rules and regulations (_vinaya_).

The Dïgha-Nikáya explains the history of Buddhism in relation to the Sangha, kings and general public alike. It discusses the origin of the ethical, social, and political phenomena of Buddhism, the beginning of ideological problems within the Sangha and the attempts for a solution. This solution was derived solely from the use of democratic principles which are the basis of Buddhist moral philosophy.

---

[21]"O Evil One! I shall not pass away until my monks will be disciples and erudite; and follow accordingly my teachings (_dhamma_), until they can teach or make known my sublime law (_dhamma_) to others and can confute any counter-teaching, and until my divine life is prosperous and widely spread and manifest by Gods (_devas_) and human beings." Bhikkhu J. Kashyap, Gen. ed., The Anguttara Nikáya (Chakkanipáta, Sattakanipáta & Atthakanipáta) (Bihar: Páli Publication Board, (Bihar Government), B.E. 2504/1960), p. 398.

[22]Dialogues of the Buddha (The Dïgha Nikáya), translated by T.W. and C.A.F. Rhys Davids (London: Published for the Páli Text Society by Luzac & Company, LTD., 1971), p. 184. See also Hermann Oldenberg, ed., The Vinaya Piṭakaṁ (The Mahávagga), Vol. I (London: Published for the Páli Text Society by Luzac & Company, LTD., LTD., 1964), p. XXVI.

[23]Ibid.

Moral philosophy is the first and most important step to considering the Sangha as an ideal society.

CHAPTER II

BUDDHIST MORAL PHILOSOPHY

As a background for studying the Sangha, one must first understand the basic structure of Buddhist ethics, which is moral conduct (sīla). Morality is not only the foundation on which the Sangha is based, but also the principle which governs it in a democratic way. Without morality the Sangha can not be an ideal society, nor can it function properly. The Buddha showed morality as essential for leading a harmonious and religious life not only for the Sangha, but also for the rest of society. He never said, "One rule is for the individual and another for the society." Nor did he say, "Ethical principle is different from political principle."

Ethics is fundamental to Buddhist practice. This Buddhist concept of ethical conduct, or "sīla", has a number of meanings in English. Virtue,[1] morality or precept,[2] morals,[3] moral habit,[4] and ethics[5] are some of the English translations of this word. T.W. Rhys Davids and William Stede have described how the term sīla is used in Páli. Sīla appeared in the Buddhist texts[6] with various prefixes

---

[1]Dhammapada (Text and Translation) by Venerable Acharya Buddharakkhita Thera (Bangalore: Buddha Vacana Trust, Maha Bodhi Society, 1966), 16:9.

[2]Richard F. Gombrich, Precept and Practice (Oxford University Press, 1971), p. 244.

[3]The Book of the Gradual Sayings (Anguttara-Nikáya), Vol. I, translated by F.L. Woodward (London: Published for the Páli Text Society by Luzac & Company, LTD., 1960), p. 247.

[4]The Middle Length Sayings (Majjhima-Nikáya), Vol. I, translated by I.B. Horner (London: Published for the Páli Text Society by Luzac & Company, LTD., 1954), p. 363.

[5]The Samyutta-Nikáya of the Sutta-Piṭaka, Part I (London: Published for the Páli Text Society by Messrs. Luzac & Company, LTD., 1960), p. 141.

[6]Páli-English Dictionary (London: Published by the Páli Text Society, 2494/1950), pp. 171-172.

and suffixes, each of which bears a specific meaning. For example, Susīla means a good character, or good behavior. Dussīla means an immoral or bad character, while vádasīla is a bellicose or quarrelsome nature. Sīlakkhandha implies an aggregate of moral conduct, while sīlasampadá suggests a good character. Cittasīla means the cultivation of mind, damanasīla is one who conquers, and párisuddhasīla translates as one of a perfectly pure character. Sīla itself is also described as sikkhápadáni, trainings, or preliminary conditions to any higher spiritual development. Examples are pañca sīla (five precepts),[7] atthangasīla (eight precepts), dasa sīla (ten precepts), pátimokkhasīla (227 disciplinary rules of bhikkhus or monks)[8] and so on. Thus, Sīla in Buddhism is good quality of character, the rules of behavior, or a set of moral rules which a person undertakes to practice for a purpose.

In contrast to the usual western understanding of moral rules, i.e., sīla is not a universal obligation or divine commandments, but rather it is a religious moral standard applied particularly within a group of followers and generally to all of mankind. Its main emphasis is on practical religious values rather than on abstract dialectical methods. Buddhist ethical conduct (sīla) stresses genuine tolerance, benevolence, consideration, love, sympathy, good-will, moderation, generosity, and far-sightedness. Hence, any altruistic value is part of the code. These genuine virtues are the cornerstones of humanistic behavior. In short, one could say that "to avoid all evil, to cultivate good, and to purify one's mind" is the aim of Buddhist ethical practice.[9]

In the west, the word "ethics" usually refers to consistent systems of moral principles which deal in a sophisticated way with right and wrong. These systems attempt to deal with justice and injustice, and the good and bad of human behavior. In general, western systems of ethics may be divided into consequentialist and intentionalist schools. The consequentialist focuses on the results of action or behavior and determines the action as good or bad according

---

[7]See The Negative Aspects of Ethical Conduct below.

[8]Cf. Somdech Phra Maha Samana Chao Kron Phraya Vajirañánavarorasa's The Entrance to the Vinaya (Vinayamukha) Vol. I.

[9]Dhammapada (Text and Translation) by Venerable Acharya Buddharakkhita, 14:5.

to its results, regardless of its intention or motive. The intentionalist in contrast, holds that motives make the act good or bad, regardless of its consequence.

In Buddhism, the concept of sīla encompasses all of these aspects. The motive is one thing and the act is another and its result is still another. For example, a person intending to kill a foe gives him poison, but by mistake, it happens to be a vitamin. Conversely, a physician intending to cure his patient gives medication that by mistake is a poison and his patient dies. In either of these cases, the nature of the intention was different from the nature of the action performed. The result in either case was undesired. One person's intention was vicious but resulted in good whereas the other person's intention was noble, but resulted in evil. Buddhist ethics account for both intention and result as good or bad separately. Therefore, sīla is the rule which produces kusalakamma (good cause and effect of action) and it is also the character trait which results from following these rules.

Ethico-Psychological Causality and Class Mobility

The Buddhist view of karma (kamma in Pāli) (i.e., the cause and effect of action) holds that any action that involves karma is conjoined with volition (cetaná). Action (kamma) without volition is morally neutral and it is neither good nor evil. Wind blowing, fire burning, water flowing, earthquakes shaking (i.e, natural phenomena) are not considered karma. Similarly, human action without cetaná is not regarded as karma.

For example, the venerable monk, Cakkhupála, who was blind, destroyed many insects while walking about performing his meditation (cankamante). He did not have cetaná or the volition to kill any insect; nonetheless, his act resulted in the destruction of many animals. When other monks saw this destruction (pāṇa) and reported it to the Buddha, he said,

> ...Yath'eva tumhe tan na passatha, tathá so pi te
> páṇe na passati, khïṇásavánan maranacetaná náma
> natthi bhikkhave'ti.[10]

Thus, the fact that the blind monk killed many insects was not regarded as bad karma because there was no intention (cetaná) to kill. Another example, according to the Pátimokkha rules, concerns a monk who deliberately emits semen. It is a Sanghádisesa offence, while emission of semen during a dream is no offence. The Buddha said, "sancetaniká sukkavisatthi aññatra supinantá saṁghádiseso'ti."[11] Therefore, an action without volition (cetaná) is not karma.

Hence, cetaná is the primary mental state for all conscious action. It can be roused by internal or external factors to lead one to action or it can initiate actions in the mind, which in turn lead to actions of body and speech, and therefore itself is part of karma. As a result, karmic act is either moral or immoral. Thus an immoral act starts with an unwholesome intention (akusala cetaná) and a moral act with the opposite kind of intention (kusala cetaná). In other words, when an action is motivated by any mental impurity, it is unwholesome in contrast to an action motivated by wholesome thoughts which therefore is good.

According to Buddhist philosophy, such unwholesome actions derive from the following conditions: (1) Lust or greed (lobha), hatred (dosa), (3) delusion (moha), (4) illogical thought (ayonisomanasikára) and (5) misdirected thought (micchápaṇihitam cittaṁ). These are the primary conditions for committing evil acts. If these conditions did not exist, then there would be no intentional acts of evil, or dishonest behavior. In the absence of these conditions unwholesome behavior could not exist. The same relationship between action and condition is true for good acts and honest or wholesome behavior. The good mental qualities

---

[10]"As you did not see him (Cakkhupála killing), so also did he not see those insects. O monks! a person whose mental defilements have been eradicated (khïṇásavánan) has no intention to kill." Dhammapadaṭṭhakathá (The Commentary on the Dhammapada), Vol. I, p. 20.

[11]"The intentional emission of semen except in a dream is a Sanghádisesa offence." Hermann Oldenberg, ed., The Vinaya Piṭakaṁ (The Suttavibhanga), Vol. III (london: Published for the Páli Text Society by Luzac & Company, LTD., 1964), p. 112.

from which good acts derive are these: (1) non-greed or generosity (alobha), (2) non-anger or loving thought (adosa), non-delusion or wisdom (amoha), (4) proper attention to the ethical path (yonisomanasikára), (5) and rightly directed thought (sammápaníhitam cittam).[12]

These causes and conditions, however, are themselves also the results of actions. A cause (hetu paccayá) produces an effect and in turn an effect can become a cause. This may be described as vipáka paccayá. In the broad sense, this concept can be explained as the acorn\oak, or egg\chicken, phenomenon. An oak tree produces acorns and a chicken produces eggs; in turn an oak tree grows out of an acorn and a chicken from an egg. The oak and the chicken can become conditions for some other result, i.e., in turn the chicken can be used for food and the oak for wood for cooking the chicken. Everything has its cause and effect, and it is sufficient and scientific to describe things in this way. Furthermore in Buddhist belief, all that has origin has cessation. Buddhism says this cause and effect and this cessation is absolutely without exception. No other religious or philosophical system, (or any system whatsoever) can fully explain this point reasonably and clearly without making any exception. However, according to Buddhism, if there is an exception, then there is a gap in the cause and effect relation. The Buddha said,

Iti imasmiṁ sati idaṁ hoti imassuppádá idaṁ uppajjati imasmiṁ asati idaṁ na hoti imassa nirodhá idam nirujjhati.[13]

This is the nature of the "causal" relation in Buddhism. An action can become a cause (kammapaccayá). Even nothingness can become a cause or condition (natthipaccayá). Anything that happened before (purejáta) can become

---

[12]E. Hardy, ed., The Anguttara-Nikáya, Vol. V (London: Published for the Páli Text Society by Luzac & Company, LTD., 1958), pp. 86-87.

[13]"Thus, this being, that comes to be; from the arising of this, that arises; this not being, that does not come to be; from the ceasing of this, that is ceased." M. Leon Feer, ed., The Samyutta-Nikáya, Part II (London: Published for the Páli Text Society by Luzac & Company, LTD., 1960), p. 28.

a cause. Similarly, anything that happened later (pacchájáta)[14] can also become a cause or condition for something else.

The momentary or impermanent conditions or factors of consciousness form potentiality (bïja) as subliminal consciousness. This subliminal series of consciousness flowing in an uninterrupted way gives rise to the consciousness of identity.[15] In terms of genesis, at the time when consciousness comes into being, so also is substantiality born.[16] By this it is meant that although mentality is born prior to the materiality, mentality is possible only if there is materiality. In the same way, mental action (manokamma) creates physical actions and vice versa. Thus, there is an explanation as to why good and evil acts are committed, and why there is right and wrong behavior: there is a seamless relationship between them. The Buddha said,

> Manopubbangamá dhammá manoseṭṭhá manomayá;
> manasá ce paduṭṭhena bhásati vá karoti vá, tato
> naṁ dukkhamanveti cakkaṁ'va vahato padaṁ.

> Manopubbangamá dhammá manoseṭṭhá manomayá;
> manasá ce pasannena bhásati vá karoti vá, tato naṁ
> sukhamanveti cháyá'va anapáyinï.[17]

---

[14]Bhikkhu J. Kashyap, General ed., The Paṭṭhána, Part IV (Bihar: Pali Publication Board, Bihar Government, B.E. 2505/1961), pp. 14-15; see also Bhikkhu J. Kashyap General ed., The Paṭṭhána, Part I (Bihar: Páli Publication Board, Bihar Government, B.E. 2505/1961), p. 105.

[15]Professor P. Lakshmi Narasu, What is Buddhism, third edition (Calcutta: Published by Davapriya Valisinha, Mahabodhi Society of India, 1964), p. 87.

[16]The Expositor (Atthasálinï), Vol. I, translated by Pe Maung Tin (London: The Páli Text Society, 1958), p. 49.

[17](1) "Mind precedes all unwholesome states and is their chief; they are all mind-wrought. If with an impure mind a person speaks or acts, misery follows him like the wheel that dogs the foot of the ox. (2) Mind precedes all wholesome states and is their chief; they are all mind-wrought. If with a pure mind a person speaks or acts, happiness follows him like his never-departing shadow."

16

Thought is what human beings are about. Thought is the primary source of all things (this is another interpretation of dhamma).[18] It is the forerunner and chief of all things. To paraphrase the Buddha, the mind (thought) is foremost (manosetthá). Everything is created by the mind (manomayá). Accordingly, if an action is performed with good volition or intention (cetaná) the results are favorable. If the intentions are bad the results are bad.

According to the Dhammapada Commentary, the word "mano", as in manosetthá or manomayá, seems to comprise the meaning of all wholesome thoughts pertaining to the realm of the senses (kámávacara kusala citta).[19] Evil thoughts (akusala citta) and neutral thoughts (abyákata citta) were concerned with four realms (catubhúmika).[20] Thoughts or mental phenomena are light (lahutá), easily pliable (mudutá) and therefore come ahead (pubbangamá) of all physical actions in planning and carrying out any act. All things resulting from thoughts are dominated or ruled by thoughts. Every experience, being the consequence of thought, follows (anveti) the thinker. Therefore, the thought or intention is the foundation for a karmic act.

Karma is a natural law governed by no supreme being. According to Buddhism, there is no such being to dispense rewards or punishments. In The

---

Dhammapada (Text and Translation) by Venerable Acharya Buddharakkhita Thera (Bangalore: Buddha Vacana Trust, Maha Bodhi Society, 2510/1966), 1:1-2.

[18]Different translators have given different meanings for the word "dhamma," such as creatures (Albert J. Edmunds), natures (S. Radhakrishnan) and, all that we are (F. Xax Muller). We can safely conclude that "dhamma" carries the meaning of both physical and mental phenomena.

[19]The Commentary on the Dhammapada, Vol. I, edited by H.C. Norman (London: Published for the Páli Text Society by Luzac & Company, LTD., 1970), p. 21: "Tattha mano'ti kámávacarakusaládibhedána catubhúmikacittan."

[20]The four realms are: (a) realm of the senses (kámabhúmi), (b) form realm (rúpabhúmi), (c) formless realm (arúpabhúmi), (d) and supra-mundane realm (lokuttarabhúmi). Dhamma Vibhága Numerical Sayings of Dhamma, Part Two, p. 79.

Anguttara-Nikáya, the Buddha addressed the monks saying that a monk should continuously contemplate the fact that

> Kammassako'mhi kammadáyádo kammayoni kammabandhu kammapatisarano, yaṁ kammaṁ karissámi kalyánaṁ vá pápakaṁ vá, tassa dáyádo bhavissámi`ti.[21]

Karma cannot be avoided. It produces results just as a living seed produces a plant under the right conditions. Good action brings happiness and evil action suffering (dukkha). In other words, "As you sow, so shall you reap" is the notion of karma.

Thus, from this understanding of karma we can see and that ethics and karma are inseparable. When we talk about actions, ethics is implicit. One who intentionally performs good actions necessarily has moral conduct. Similarly, one who deliberately performs bad deeds has a bad character. His outcome tends to be unpleasant. Ethics and karma are as two sides of the same coin and cannot be judged one without the other. Without ethics, karma is bad and without action (karma), ethics has no basis for explanation or value.

According to Buddhist philosophy, everything is impermanent and is constantly changing. Everything has three stages, evolution into being, sustenance, and cessation. This philosophy of impermanence explains the principle of class mobility, which states that a man is a free being. There is no Supreme Being or Agency responsible for his existence, or condition of that existence. A man is the master of his own destiny. "Who else can be your master?"[22] asked the Buddha. Buddhist philosophy tells us that good or bad change can take place based on actions. This idea of ethico-psychological causality is deeply ingrained in the

---

[21]"I am the creator of my own actions (kammassakomhi). Actions are my heir (kammadáyádo). I am born according to my actions (kammayoni). I have relatives (kammabandhu) because of my actions, and actions are my refuge (kammapatisarano). Actions I performed, whether good or bad will determine my inheritance." E. Hardy,. ed., The Anguttara-Nikáya, Part V (London: Published for the Páli Text Society by Luzac & Company, LTD., 1958), p. 88.

[22]The Dhammapada, 12:4.

Buddhist concept of class mobility or change of a person's status. We can see then how the law of karma has its implications in this idea of class mobility.

In order to understand clearly the relationship between the law of karma and human development or class mobility, we must first consider the general implications of both. Buddhists are prompted by the concept of ethico-psychological causality when they try to overcome a particular state of existence or when they strive to reach one. Those who are propelled by this concept realize that they control their own fate and act accordingly. Ethical behavior has a positive impact on the Buddhist religio-social community during a person's life time, karma explains the connection between one life and the next. It is that which explains the inequality of the existences. The more one contemplates this idea, the subtler the kammic result will appear. In this way, an ignoble pauper can become a noble, wealthy person (and vice versa) through his actions (kamma) and other factors.

The glaring inequality between human beings is everywhere evident. Some people are intelligent, or healthy, or well-to-do; they may also be attractive and live long lives. On the other hand, some people are illiterate, sick, and quite poor; they in turn may be unattractive and die at an early age. What is the source of this inequality or biased destination? How can this inequality exist among the human race? To this question people express many different opinions. The answer may involve religious, psychological, biological, philosophical, social, economic, political, geographical or other reasons. One of these reasons alone may not be a sufficient and reasonable answer to this question.

According to Buddhist principles, all these reasons together or separately can explain human inequality. For example, it is believed that a humble nature may lead to high social status, or jealousy may result in a low social status. Human beings are of a complex nature and this problem of inequality is therefore infinitely complex and abstruse. Different religions make claims about this significant question from their own perspectives. All Indian philosophies except Carvaka explain it by taking into account previous births and believe that those who have committed a bad karma in a past life are suffering the karmic results in the present life. Buddhists strongly believe that each individual has had innumerable lives and will have innumerable rebirths as long as he has not attained enlightenment (nirvána), which cannot happen while mental impurities are present. That nirvána is where the cause and effect (karma) ceases.

As stated before, according to Buddhism, the inequality which exists amongst humans is a result of each individual's actions. The Buddha's response to the questions by the Brahman youth Subha, a son of Todeyya, attempted to explain why inequality existed amongst human beings. To paraphrase the Cullakammavibhanga Sutta[23] which contains his answer: (1) one person is ugly, deformed, or of low social status. (2) Another person is also ugly, deformed, but opulent. (3) Still another person may be beautiful but impoverished, and of a low social status. (4) And yet, another person may possess everything (beauty, wealth, high social position, etc.). The Buddha further explained that people of an ill-tempered nature who were vengeful and easily provoked would be subsequently ugly and deformed in another life. Jealousy and stinginess in a prior life would result in a present life of poverty and low status. On the other hand, another individual with the same ill-temper and vengeful nature in a previous life could be wealthy in his present life as a result of his generosity in a prior life. Another person may now have a high social status in his present life in spite of poor behavior before. Still another person having had good temper and patience previously may be handsome or lovely in the present state. However if this same handsome or lovely person was not generous in his prior life, he may now be poor. In the same way, a person having had a good temper, a mild manner and a non-vengeful nature in a previous existence will today be an attractive, rich individual of high status. This is the manner in which the Buddha explained the inequality of humans.

It is clear that being wealthy is the result of past generosity, while poverty is born out of stinginess. However, this point must not be taken naively or lightly. A thorough investigation must be made of each situation. Not all well-to-do or bourgeois individuals are enjoying the result of a previously performed good karma. Nor are all poor people suffering fate from a past negative karma. Hence, a person's life is not only determined by deeds in the past, but also by corruption and similar illegal or immoral dealings in the present. Likewise, despite working hard, poverty can still prevail in individuals' lives if they are suppressed and tyrannized by rich people or unjust government. Obviously, such a state of economic inequality and cruel conditions is social injustice. Therefore, we must not try to

---

[23]The Middle Length Sayings (Majjhima-Nikáya), Vol. III, translated from the Páli by I.B. Horner (London: Published for the Páli Text Society by Luzac & Company, LTD., 1967), pp. 248-253.

justify it by falsely making use of the principle of karma, the moral causation, every time.

> The rich might have slaughtered economically, and consequently politically and morally, millions of their brethren before they reached places of social eminence they now occupy and enjoy to the full extent... They are privileged to live upon the sweat and blood of others, who know not where to lay their heads, and who are daily succumbing to the heavy burden, not of their free choice, but forced upon them by society.[24]

Thus, our life and society are conditioned by various factors. Nevertheless, our actions are one of the leading factors that can bring about the evolution of an unsatisfactory situation into a good one and vice versa. According to the Buddha, one's actions or karma determine one's future, but there are always complex ethical implications in so far as the inequality of human beings is concerned. Only the state of nibbána is beyond any good or bad karma.

Buddhist philosophy further states that belief in a Supreme Being is a false view (micchádiṭṭhi). Buddhism encourages the individual to put stock in his own actions (kamma). The individual becomes self-reliant when he realizes that everything he experiences, whether good or bad, is the result of his past behavior. A person learns to make the best of any situation. When he feels happy, he recognizes that this feeling is a result of a good karma and he strives to increase his happiness by performing even more good deeds. A bad day is accepted as the result of a past karma. This person boldly undergoes any suffering. His determination allows him to accept his punishment. He blames neither a god, nor another person. Likewise, he thanks no one, and praises no Supreme Being for his happiness.

Those who believe in karma are supposed to do good deeds and abandon evil ones since their aim is to obtain favorable results in the future if not in the

---

[24]Daisetz Teitaro Suzuki, Outlines of Maháyána Buddhism (New York: Schocken Books, 1963), p. 188.

present life. Hence, they are quite optimistic. Persons who believe this think that if karma has results in a future existence, then he shall be happy in future because he has done good and been benevolent in the present. But if by chance there is no other world, no fruition of karma, no rebirth, he can accept that too. He has nothing to fear, nor anything to worry about, because he has done no wrong and is happy in his present life too. This self-confidence is the direct result of observing good moral practices.

Those who do not believe in karma may behave contrary to the ethical values. They may think that their actions will not affect them in the future but bring only happiness and enjoyment in the present life. Their actions may even disturb the peace and harmony of society since they are performed for selfish reasons and not according to ethical values. Although these people do not believe in karma, in fact their actions are karma (and explained by this natural law).

While preaching the law of karma, the Buddha indicated the outcome of class mobility. He told King Pasenadi that there were ultimately four separate classes of people:

> Tamo tama-paráyano, tamo joti-paráyano;
> Joti tama-paráyano, joti joti-paráyano hoti.[25]

In other words, in the ebb and flow of human inequality which is the consequence of karma, people finally will fall into one of these classes. The first category represents the type of person who, due to past deeds, lives in a family of low social and economic status. This person is usually ill-fed, dwells in wretched conditions and associates with immoral characters. He probably has various physical defects and diseases. Education and ethical values are foreign to him. He is lazy and motivated by evil thoughts, words and deeds. The consequences of his actions lead him to even more misery. He staggers from one blindness to the next, from one darkness to another.

---

[25]"(i) Those that are joined to darkness and move to darkness. (ii) Those that are joined to darkness and move to light. (iii) Those that are joined to light and move to darkness. (iv) Those that are joined to light and move to light." M. Leon Feer, ed. The Samyutta-Nikáya of the Sutta-Piṭaka, Part I, p. 93; see The Book of the Kindred Sayings (Samyutta-Nikáya), Part I, p. 118.

The second category also represents a person born into poor circumstances. However, this individual actively works to be good. Happily, this effort yields only positive results. He may be physically defective and the possibility of improving his personal appearance and social status is more likely. The affirmative opportunities that flow his way are the result of his good efforts.

The third category concerns a person born into a family of wealth, power, and high social status. He is healthy, wealthy and possibly handsome. However, in spite of his favorable condition, he prefers to cling to evil in every way. As a result, he meets with disaster, thereby losing everything he had: his name, fame, reputation, and pride. Hence, he moves from light toward darkness.

The last category represents a successful person. Born into favorable circumstances, he is honest and positive in his words, deeds and actions. As a result of his moral behavior, he reaps felicitous benefits.[26] His world is infinitely bright.

This same pattern of personal ethics can be applied to national class mobility. That is to say, if every citizen is conscientious, hard working, and of a strong moral will, then the nation itself will be the same.

In summary then, we must trust ourselves in our own ability to create or destroy the world. The Buddha said, "By effort one overcomes suffering (viriyena dukkhaṁ acceti)."[27]

In The Path of Purification, Buddhaghosa defines the function of morality or ethical conduct, as:

---

[26]Ibid., pp. 118-120.

[27]M. Leon Feer, ed., The Samyutta-Nikáya of the Sutta-Piṭaka, Part I (London: Published for the Páli Text Society by Messrs. Luzac & Company, LTD., 1960), p. 214.

Dussilyaviddhansanatá,   anavajjagunotathá
Kiccasampatti-atthena raso náma pavuccati.[28]

Buddhist ethical conduct has two aspects, one positive and one negative. The negative aspect prohibits man from engaging in unethical or immoral behavior. The positive aspect requires that he perform altruistic deeds.

The Negative Aspects of Ethical Conduct

The basic ethical code of prohibition for all Buddhists is:

    1. Pánátipátá veramani sikkhápadam samádiyámi.
        2.   Adinnádáná   veramani   sikkhápadam samádiyámi.
        3.   Kámesu   micchácárá   veramani sikkhápadam samádiyámi.
        4.   Musávádá   veramani   sikkhápadam samádiyámi.
        5. Surámeraya majjapamádatthaná veramani sikkhápadam   samádiyámi.[29]

These are the five ethical precepts (pañca síla) which all Buddhists are advised to practice. These precepts are the foundation for all moral principles but there are

---

[28]Henry Clarke Warren, ed., Visuddhimagga of Buddhaghosácariya revised by Dharmánanda Kosambi (Cambridge: Harvard University Press, 1950), p. 8. The quoted passage is translated as "Action to stop misconduct, then Achievement as the quality, blamelessness in (a) virtuous man:" Bhadantácáriya Buddhaghosa, The Path of Purification (Visuddhimagga), translated by Bhikkhu Nanamoli (Ceylon: Published by R. Semage, Colombo, 1956), p. 8.

[29]1. I undertake the training rule to restrain from killing any living beings. 2. I undertake the training rule to restrain from taking anything that is not given to me. 3. I undertake the training rule to restrain from sexual misconduct. 4. I undertake the training rule to restrain from false speech. 5. I undertake the training rule to restrain from taking intoxicants.

more rules (the Vinaya) for monks that are even more stringent. Thus, in Buddhist countries lay people voluntarily vow to obey the five major precepts against killing, stealing, sexual misconduct, false speech and intoxicating substances.

Various conditions (sambhāra) must exist for it to be determined that one has violated one of these precepts. In other words, if one of these conditions does not exist then it is considered that the precept has not been violated completely.

For example, five conditions (sambhāra)[30] must exist in order to transgress the rule about killing. They are: (1) the existence of an actual living being, (2) the knowledge by a person that it is a living being, (3) the intention of killing it, (4) the attack or effort to kill it, (5) and that (by his effort) the living being has really died.

The five sambhāra[31] necessary for the act of stealing are: (1) the existence of an object belonging to another person, (2) the thief realizing that it belongs to another person, (3) the intention of stealing it, (4) the effort (upakkama) to steal it and (5) the acquisition of that possession. If these five sambhāra exist then stealing is a wrong action.

Sexual misbehavior consists of the sexual union between a man and woman who are not legally joined in marriage.[32] This misconduct usually results in making enemies. The Buddha explained that four misfortunes befell a careless person who committed adultery: the person acquires demerits and a negative destiny; his sleep is disturbed; he is blamed for the transgression, and he

---

[30]T.W. Rhys Davids and J. Estlin Carpenter, eds., The Sumangala-Vilāsini, Buddhaghosa's Commentary on the Dïgha-Nikáya, Part I (second edition) (London: Published for the Páli Text Society by Luzac & Company, LTD., 1968), pp. 69-70.

[31]T.W. Rhys Davids and J. Estlin Carpenter, eds., The Sumangala-Vilāsini, Buddhaghosa's Commentary on the Dïgha-Nikáya, Part I, p. 71.

[32]It is interesting to note that neither text nor commentary mentioned how many sambhāra were involved in order to count complete transgression of this precept.

encounters a state of woe. The king also imposed a heavy punishment. Hence, the Buddha warned that a man should not covet another's wife.[33]

False speech occurs when a person intentionally utters misleading statements, or purposefully misinforms another person. In Buddhism, the four sambhára[34] for violating the precept on false speaking are: (1) a person possessing knowledge that something spoken is untrue, (2) the intention of giving someone false information, (3) an effort to do such a thing, (4) and an innocent person's being deceived by the false information. False speech entails other forms of communication, not just the verbal kind. Body language can also be used to disseminate false ideas. Winks, nods, gesticulations, and other body movements can affect[35] what people believe in certain situations. When someone is intentionally misdirected or misinformed by someone else these acts, too, are considered a part of false speech.

The Positive Aspects of Ethical Conduct

Abstaining from immoral acts is merely a preliminary stage to moral practice. This practice is considered to be developed only when the person engages in altruistic behavior, which is the positive aspect of ethics. This positive development involves the effort to do all kinds of good acts in body, mind, and speech. Hence, the simple avoidance of immoral acts is not morally sufficient.

---

[33]The Dhammapada, 21:4-5.

[34]The Sumangala-Vilásini, Buddhaghosa's Commentary on the Dïgha-Nikáya, Part I, p. 72.

[35]Somdetch Phra Maha Samana Chao Krom Phraya Vajirañánavarorasa, The Entrance to the Vinaya (Vinayamukha), Vol. I (Bangkok: Mahámakutarájavidyálaya, 2512/1969), p. 37.

The classical positive aspects of ethical conduct in Buddhism are the "four divine abodes" (brahma-vihára).[36] These abodes are (1) loving-kindness (mettá) -- the desire for others' happiness, (2) compassion (karuná) -- the motivation to help release others from suffering, pain and dissatisfaction, (3) sympathetic joy (mudità) -- the joy one feels when one sees good fortune coming to others, and (4) equanimity (upekkhá) -- even mindedness. These qualities are also called the dwelling places of the Great Ones.[37] The mind of a person having these qualities becomes free of hindrances (nïvarana) through the practice of brahma-vihára. A scripture, The Path of Purification appearing about 1700 years ago, gives many details of the four brahma-viháras[38] as the classical notion of the positive aspects of moral philosophy.

Loving-kindness (mettá), an essential virtue in Buddhist ethics is also one of the ten perfections (páramitá,[39] dasa páramïyo)[40] (or qualities to strive for)

---

[36]In the Abhidhamma, the brahma-vihára is described as appamaññá or infinitude of philanthropy. See Bhikkhu J. Kashyap, General Editor, The Vibhanga (Bihar Government: Páli Publication Board, B.E. 2504/1960), pp. 332 ff.

[37]Vajirañánavarorasa, Navakováda, p. 47.

[38]Bhadantácáriya Buddhaghosa, The Path of Purification (Visudhimagga), Vol. I, translated from Páli by Bhikkhu Nyanamoli (California: Shambhala Publication Inc., Berkeley, 1976), p. 321 ff.

[39]Woven Cadences of early Buddhists (Sutta-Nipata), translated by E. M. Hare (London: Oxford University Press, 1947), p. 146; see also Richard Morris, Dr. Georg Landsbeg and Mrs. Rhys Davids eds., Puggala-Paññatti and Atthakathá (London: Published for the Páli Text Society by Messrs. Luzac & Company, LTD., 1972), p. 70.

[40]V. Fausboll, The Játaka together with its Commentary being Tales of the Anterior Births of Gotama Buddha, Vol. I (London: Published for the Páli Text Society by Messrs. Luzac & Company, LTD., 1962), p. 73; H.C. Norman, ed., Dhammapadatthakathá, Vol. I (London: Published for the Páli Text Society by Luzac & Company, LTD., 1970), p. 84: The ten perfections (dasa-páramïyo) are: (1) giving or liberality (dána), (2) morality (sïla), (3) renunciation (nekkhamma), (4) wisdom (paññá), (5) energetic effort (viriya), (6) forbearance (khanti), (7)

in Theravāda Buddhism which are given in later Páli literature.   T h e s e
perfections are practiced as ideal principles by sages in order to obtain their goals
of nibbána. The Buddha, who was the epitome of ethical conduct in his many
lives, taught all his lessons out of loving-kindness (mettá) and compassion
(karuná) in order to liberate human beings and Gods from the sufferings of cyclical
existence.

The Buddha's heart was so filled with loving-kindness and compassion that
he tamed the cruel murderer, Angulimála,[41] the fearsome Nálágiri elephant and
Nandopananda, the serpent.[42] Through these examples of the power of the
Buddha's mettá, we can understand that bereft of mettá, Buddhism would not offer
a means to perfect peace and tranquility. Hence, if a person has no mettá for
others, then it is not possible for him to abstain from hurting or killing living
beings. The very nature of practicing moral precepts involves the cultivation of
mettá for others. In fact, the whole religio-ethical core of Buddhism and humanity
is based upon mettá and karuná. In addition to being an essential quality to strive
for, loving-kindness (mettá) is used as a meditation subject to cultivate the
mind.[43] A bhikkhu dwells in meditation, spreading his unlimited loving thought
(mettá-sahagatena cetasá) throughout the universe for all living beings. Thus, by

---

truth (sacca), (8) resolution (addhitthána), (9) love or loving-kindness (mettá),
(10) equanimity (upekkhá).

[41]The Middle Length Sayings (Majjhima-Nikáya), Vol. II, translated by I.B.
Horner (London: Published for the Páli Text Society by Luzac & Company, LTD.,
1957), pp. 284 ff.

[42]Bhikshu Buddhaghosha Mahasthavir, ed., Paritrána (With Introduction and
Meaning) (Yala: Subhasha Printing Press, 2527/1983), pp. 43-44.

[43]Bhadantácariya Buddhaghosa, The Path of Purification (Visuddhimagga),
translated from the Páli by Bhikkhu Nyanamoli (2nd edition) (Colombo: Published
by A Semage, 1964), pp. 98 ff.

28

this practice, he obtains freedom or liberation of thought through loving-kindness (mettá ceto-vimutti).[44]

There is a difference between the quality or virtue of mettá and karuná, the second divine abode. Mettá is usually used by someone to help individuals in general when they are facing some adversity, while Karuná is applied to help individuals who are naturally low in spirit or capability. Therefore, someone else's help is necessary to overcome the situation in karuná. However, mettá and karuná, or dayá, are complementary to each other and are applied to non-human beings as well. For example, a potter's son, the monk, Dhaniya, built his hut wholly with kneaded mud. The Buddha rebuked him by saying, "na hi náma bhikkhave tassa moghapurisassa pánesu anuddayá anukampá avihesá bhavissati."[45] When one kneads mud it is inevitable that a lot of small creatures will be destroyed. Buddhaghosa's explanation says that when anuddayá is aroused in a person, he is moved to protect beings beforehand and then to exhibit the nature of loving-kindness (mettá-pubbabhávam dasseti) by helping or protecting. This compassion is anuddayá or anukampá, which moves one's heart to recognize other beings' suffering (paradukkhena cittakampaná).[46]

One who has karuná also has mudiṫá, another of the four divine abodes. Mudiṫá is the appreciative joy[47] which arises in the heart at perceiving the success of others. "Congratulations" and like sayings are the expression of mudiṫá, the pure

---

[44]T.W. Rhys Davids and J. Estlin Carpenter, eds., The Dïgha-Nikáya, Vol. I (London: Published by the Páli Text Society, 1975), p. 251.

[45]"O monks! that foolish man has no iota of pity (anuddayá), nor an iota of compassionate thought (anukampá) for not hurting living beings." Hermann Oldenberg, ed., The Vinaya-Pitakam (The Suttavibhanga), Vol. III (London: Published for the Páli Text Society by Luzac & Company, LTD., 1964), p. 42.

[46]J. Takakusu and M. Nagai, eds., Samantapásádiká Buddhaghosa's Commentary on the Vinaya Pitaka, Vol II (London: Published for the Páli Text Society by Luzac & Company, LTD., 1969), p. 288.

[47]Narada Maha Thera, ed. & tr., A Manual of Abhidhamma Being Abhidhammattha Sangaha of Bhadanta Anuruddhácariya (Colombo: Buddhist Publication Society, 1968), pp. 131-132.

sympathy, happiness or gentleness of heart. A bhikkhu with a good heart dwells in meditation by spreading not only his thoughts of loving-kindness (mettá) but also thoughts of sympathetic joy (muditá-sahagatena cetasá ... pharitvá viharati).[48] Furthermore, Muditá is one of the important mental factors which eradicates envy and aversion.[49] By repeatedly practicing and developing muditá, one can attain liberation, or freedom of thought (muditá ceto-vimutti),[50] or the state of nirvána.

In addition to the three divine abodes of mettá, karuná and muditá, there is upekkhá, the last, but not the least, important positive virtue. It is a detached and neutral feeling, equanimity of mind. The usual implication is that upekkhá is present in one's heart when one is neither pleased (somanassa) nor displeased (domanassa);[51] neither sorrowful (adukkha) nor happy (asukha).[52] It is not the inoperativeness of mind but rather the balance. Upekkhá operates in such a way that harm comes neither to oneself nor to others. This equanimity is an even more abstract happiness (upekkhá sukha),[53] since chronologically speaking, after showing sympathetic joy (muditá), one experiences upekkhá.

---

[48]T.W. Rhys Davids and J. Estlin Carpenter, eds., The Dïgha-Nikáya, Vol. I, p. 251; J. Estlin Carpenter, ed., The Dïgha-Nikáya, Vol. III (London: Published for the Páli Text Society by Messrs. Luzac & Company, LTD., 1960), p. 30; Ibid., p. 224.

[49]See Phra Maha Singhathon Narasabho, Buddhism a Guide to a Happy Life (Bangkok: Mahachulongkornrájavidyálaya, 1971), p. 135.

[50]Ibid., pp. 248-249; see also M. Leon Feer, ed., Samyutta-Nikáya, Part V (London: Published for the Páli Text Society by Messrs. Luzac & Company, LTD., 1960), p. 118.

[51]T.W. Rhys Davids and J. Estlin Carpenter, eds., The Dïgha-Nikáya, Vol. II (London: Oxford University Press, 1947), p. 278.

[52]Estlin Carpenter, ed., The Dïgha Nikáya, Vol. III, p. 270.

[53]Richard Morris, ed., The Anguttara-Nikáya, Part I, revised by A.K. Warder (London: Published for the Páli Text Society by Luzac & Company, LTD., 1961), p. 81.

Upekkhá is one of the positive virtues that is cultivated in order to prevent oneself from over excitement in success and frustration or depression in failure. Advanced upekkhá, therefore, comes within profound meditation (jhána). Purity of mind comes through equanimity of thought (upekkhá sati párisuddhi)[54] and the meditator attains still more freedom or liberation of thought through equanimity (upekkháya ceto-vimuttiyá).[55]

These are the positive aspects of Buddhist ethics to which Theraváda followers often refer. Buddhist scholars would agree that those who are endowed with the practice of brahma-vihára can never act cruelly or violently to anybody. Clearly, a person without brahma-vihára can never be considered to be a Buddha or bodhisatva. Therefore, if one does not diffuse positive virtues for others, it is not possible to attain the ultimate goal of Buddhist ethical practice.

In addition to these four positive virtues, or divine abodes (brahma-vihára), the Buddha encouraged men to develop sober virtues in themselves. Any virtue which enables a person to obtain these goals supports morality, and therefore it can be viewed as a positive aspect of ethical conduct in Buddhism. These additional virtues cannot be neglected in considering any positive aspects of Buddhist ethical conduct.

Some of these virtues are: to know (paññá), or investigate the truth, to analyze the situation or milieu of any given condition which it is possible to know; to avoid an untrue path or pursue the truth (sacca); to stress sincerity (cága) in human relationships; to strive for peace of mind (upasama),[56] and perform our duties when our mind is calm so that we can be free from the grief that arises from things done incorrectly.

---

[54]T.W. Rhys Davids and J. Estlin Carpenter, eds., The Dïgha-Nikáya, Vol. I, p. 38.

[55]Ibid., p. 251.

[56]The Majjhima-Nikáya, Vol. III, p. 240.

When still other virtues such as iddhipáda[57] are mastered, the practitioner is led to a goal which is worthy of his effort. An attentive mind to the task concerned (citta), and the capacity to skillfully reason and investigate the particular matter (vimarhsa)[58] are some of the desirable results derived from such ethical conduct.

Finally, practicing Buddhist ethics involves forbearance (khanti) and meekness (soracca), the two-fold positive virtues.[59] Although the two are distinct, they are inseparable. Hence, khanti means tolerance, endurance or patience. (2) Soracca, means meekness, or modesty. Khanti has different levels. If a man follows this principle when he undertakes any duty, he probably stands to complete it. A man of patience never withdraws his thought and efforts from his duty. Though confronted with many obstacles, he patiently forbears such afflictions as heat, cold, rain and the like. He even endures physical and mental suffering as much as possible. He strives to complete his undertaking rather than succumb to trifling pains.

A gentle behavior can melt the hardest of minds, transforming it to a soft, pliable, and loving nature. Soracca or modesty can make beautiful any environment, whether mental or physical.

Khanti and soracca are like two sides of the same coin, giving the possessor the real value of a man. With these two ethical ideas as complements to all the other virtues, a man becomes more gentle in his behavior.

The Buddha had high expectations for his monks. He asked them to regard one another with an eye of love (mettá). He wanted his disciples to live together in a friendly and harmonious way, as milk and water blend. [Anuruddhas (the Buddha's disciples) were eager to follow mettá and the advice that they regard one

---

[57]The four iddhipádas are: 1. desire (Chanda), 2. effort (viriya), 3. attentiveness (citta), and 4. investigation (mimámsa). Somdet Phra Maha Samana Chao Krom Phraya Vajiráñánavarorasa, ed., Navakováda (Bangkok: Mahámakutarájavidyálaya, 2514/1971), p. 44; Bhikkhu J. Kashyap, General Editor, The Vibhanga, 264 ff.

[58]Vajiráñánavarorasa, Navakováda, p. 44.

[59]The Anguttara-Nikáya, Vol. I, p. 94; The Vinaya-Pitakam, Vol. I, p. 349.

another with love and respect].[60]   Thus, mettá is the essence of all positive Buddhist ethics.   It represents the basic moral tenets which every person in Buddhism should practice.   Moral values are the foundation for the religious political validity of the Sangha, which stands as the model for an ideal society.

---

[60]The Book of the Discipline (Mahávagga), Vol. IV, p. 502.

CHAPTER III

THE SANGHA AS AN IDEAL SOCIETY

The Sangha

The Sangha is the Order of fully ordained Buddhist monks (upasampadá bhikkhus), comprising a minimum of four[1] monks but having no maximum number. Circa the 6th century B.C., the Buddha founded his Sangha in northern India and led it during his life time. As we have seen in the previous chapter, in its early stages, the Sangha was a union of wandering ascetic monks who had forsaken a worldly life. They were on a path of spiritual liberation. The Buddha preached with the intention of helping them overcome their suffering (dukkha). He wanted to help them break the cycle of birth and death (saṁsára), and to attain nibbána, the ultimate goal of Buddhism. Thus, the Sangha was not cenobitical, or the organized monastic institution we have come to expect in the modern sense, with constitutional laws and regulations.

There were successive stages of development of the Sangha, namely; the ascetic stage, when contemplative recluses strove for immediate realization; the monastic stage, when unregimented monks aimed at personal perfection, or, at least, propitious rebirth; the sectarian stage, when rigid rules and orthodoxy diverted the monks' attention to pedantic competition; and finally the popular stage, when the monks sought to make their dharma available and attractive to the pious householder -- the era of a universal religion.

On the whole, the Sangha can be conceived of in two ways: (a) as a conventional (sammuti) Sangha and (b) as a noble (ariya) Sangha. The sammuti Sangha is the organized Sangha, a converted group of ordinary bhikkhus having the same type of dhamma and vinaya. They are gathered for such purposes as meditating, teaching and discussion of matters of the Sangha. One can therefore decide to become a member of a sammuti Sangha. Membership is obtained by upasampadá, ordination as a bhikkhu, and by following the laws (dhamma), and the disciplinary rules and regulations (vinaya) expounded by the Buddha. All members of the Sangha must be normal (pakatatta) bhikkhus (i.e., they must be

---

[1]A group of two to three monks is regarded as group (gaṇa), not Sangha.

ordained and morally pure). If they do not obey the same rules of the vinaya, or if through immoral actions they are exiled from the Sangha, they cannot be regarded as actual members.[2]   The ariya Sangha[3] is a group of monks who have already attained spiritual liberation [i.e., the stage of stream-enterer (sotāpanna)]. Therefore, any monk following the dhamma and vinaya who enters one of the eight noble stages (attha ariya puggala), is said to be a member of the ariya Sangha. Although these noble people have already achieved the supra-mundane stage they are still considered members of the sammuti Sangha. Hence, the Sangha is only one Sangha wherein all mundane and supra-mundane bhikkhus belong and work together. In other words, for the conventional or mundane purposes all bhikkhus are treated equally as Sangha members. And unless otherwise stated, the sammuti Sangha and ariya Sangha are not separated.

It is also important to mention that the Sangha can be viewed in two ways: as a universal Sangha, or as a particular Sangha. The universal one comprises a limitless number of members no matter where they are residing in the universe. As mentioned above, the criterion for membership is fully ordained monkhood, regardless of the personality, economic status, education, social recognition, or competency of the monks. In other words, the admittance to ordination as a full fledged monk (upasampadā bhikkhu) is the admittance of membership into the universal Sangha.

Various terms are used to determine the rank or seniority (therānuthera) of monks. The appellations are as follows: a newly ordained monk (acira-pabbajita,[4] nava or navaka bhikkhu), a middle standing (ranking) monk (majjhima bhikkhu), an elder (thera bhikkhu),[5] a great elder (mahā thera),[6] a senior monk

---

[2]See Somdet Phra Maha Samana Chao Krom Phraya Vajirañānavarorasa, compiled, The Entrance to the Vinaya Vinayamukha, Vol. III (Bangkok: Mahámakut Rájavidyálaya, 2526/1983), p. 7.

[3]Anguttara-Nikáya, Part II, p. 246.

[4]Sanyutta-Nikáya, Vol. I, p. 9.

[5]The Dïgha-Nikáya, Vol. I, p. 78; see also Anguttara-Nikáya, Part II, p. 23.

[6]The Vinaya-Piṭakaṁ: Vol. II, p. 212.

of the congregation (sangha thera),[7] a father of the Sangha (sanghapitaro), or a chief of the Sangha (sangha-náyaka). All are treated as members of the Sangha. These ranks are mainly based on duration of monkhood, practice of morality and meditation, and knowledge of dhamma and vinaya.

In most cases the leader of the Sangha is unanimously understood to be the eldest monk[8] among the group. At each gathering the number of Sangha members and its leader may vary. The hand of ecclesiastical authority is very lightly placed upon the individual members of the Sangha.

In the universal Sangha, members may or may not have communication. They may not even know how many members there are in the world, or where they dwell. There is no requirement of registration as a Sangha member, nor is there a secretarial headquarters for such purposes. When the Buddha died, there was no successor authorized to lead the Sangha. One may simply assume that monks were the members of the Sangha, although there was no such group apart from individual monks themselves. Nor is there any visible function of the universal Sangha as such because this is only an ideal Sangha which can be viewed as an ideal society.

The particular Sangha is the temporary or functional Sangha which has a fixed number of members for that particular task, time and place. In general, when the word "Sangha" is used the reader must understand that the particular Sangha (bearing a certain number of members) is the one specified. The minimum number of members is any four monks gathered in a certain place, for certain tasks, and at a certain time. The standard Sangha, which has twenty members, can carry on all kinds of formal and legitimate tasks at a given time and place within the allowance of the disciplinary rules (vinaya). In a particular Sangha there is a leader who directs the ceremony and the given tasks.

The organized Sangha administrators can be conceived of as a governmental body. The Sangha administrative body has various divisions and subdivisions of

---

[7]Ibid., p. 212; 303.

[8]In the monks' community, seniority is determined by the date and time of an individual's admission to the Sangha as a full fledged monk and not by his actual age or birth date.

officials. These officials are selected according to the nature of the work. The principal Sangha governors are classified into five main bodies according to the nature, scope, and responsibility of their duties.[9] These are: (1) food officers, (2) robe officers, (3) lodging officers, (4) áráma officers or construction supervisors, (5) and bankers or storehouse supervisors (bhandágárika).

Every group (gaṇa), organization, society, or government has certain activities in regard to its structures, maintenance, extension, or related matters. The knowledge, expertise, or skill in administering these affairs is the organization's politics. The same is true in the Sangha. The Sangha has various tasks (sanghakamma) to accomplish, such as invitation services (paváraná), dates of observance (uposatha), and the ordination of bhikkhus. The administrators must know their tasks well. If the guardian of the Sangha does not know his duties, how can he be the guardian? If the leader of the state does not know his subjects how can he be a leader? In the same way, a senior bhikkhu must know all the vinaya rules, the prescribed acts and duties of the Sangha.

Hinduism is different from Buddhism. In general, Hinduism separates different castes of people into ghettos, according to their own classifications. Buddhism does not accept the caste system. People from all classes live and operate equally with one another in and out of the Sangha. Since society is set up under a class system, people think, perform, and live by different rules. It would be impossible to regulate different classes without rules being equally applied. Therefore, the Buddha established laws (dhamma) and disciplinary rules and regulations (vinaya) so that his Sangha might run relatively independent of social obligations and secular laws.

There is no requirement of obedience to a superior, although a monk is expected to display his courtesy and respect to senior monks. In theory as well as in practice, there is seniority based on a hierarchical position within the Sangha. But ultimately speaking, all monks are individual ascetics who have not vowed obedience to anyone else but the Sangha.

---

[9]Somdet Phra Maha Samana Chao Krom Phraya Vajirañáñavarorasa, compiled, The Entrance to the Vinaya Vinayamukha, Vol. III (Bangkok: Mahámakut Rájavidyálaya Press, 2526/1983), p. 53ff.

In order to fit into the harmonious whole, one may have to adopt certain rules that lead to a desired pattern of behavior while one is in the institution of communal life. Every individual is a member of the universal Sangha. If a person acts against the established norm of behavior, then his acts show that he is an uncooperative member. He is not suited to the Sangha but is an exception to the whole. This approach is judged on the basis of rules which are democratic in nature, since they are equally applied to all.

In the gathering of the Sangha assembly, the number of members may fluctuate, but not the minimum number. In many cases, a particular Sangha can represent the universal Sangha. The smooth functioning of the Sangha is more important than the interests of an individual member. The Sangha itself is collective; whereas, the members are individuals.

The Sangha is authorized to do more than any individual member. There must be a complete quorum of the Sangha in order to legitimize formal acts and ceremonies within the group. As in any governmental office, the more competent members of the Sangha can supervise other members who need advice on how to stay in line with morality and legitimacy.

In fact, the main duty of any ecclesiastical body is to dispense wisdom, to teach, and to maintain good laws (dhamma) or disciplinary rules (vinaya). From time to time the Sangha gathers for the purpose of admonishing or clarifying the particular case of a monk who had transgressed rules, or who has been accused of violating them. The Sangha is one of the oldest continuous orders in the world. Because of the moral strength and practical reason it embodies, the Sangha can well be considered an example of an ideal society.

The Democratic Nature of the Ordination Procedure

In non-Buddhist tradition, a founder of a religion usually claims to be God, or God's messenger. In such a religion, the widest door to heaven or salvation is opened to the human being at the feet of the founder or leader. A man can never become the equal of the leader, nor can he share his power. No God, or messenger wants to share His monopoly on power. He does not entertain the possibility that a follower could become as powerful as Himself. Only God and His messenger are the Great Ones, but the followers are considered to be sinful and inferior.

In Buddhism, however, the Buddha demonstrated how he became an Enlightened Being, the Perfect Master of human and divine kinds (satthádevamanussánaṁ). The Buddha wanted to show others how to discover the way to perfection (páramitá) and to become his equal. He who completely accumulates the perfections becomes a Buddha, regardless of his prior status. Disciples who became Enlightened Ones (arahattas) after following the teaching, were shown no distinction by the Buddha between his Freedom or Enlightenment and theirs. The Buddha addressed the monks, by saying: "mutt'áhaṁ bhikkhave sabbapásehi ye dibbá ye ca mánusá. tumhe pi bhikkhave muttá sabbapásehi ye dibbá ye ca mánusá."[10] The Buddha, as well as his monks were equally arahattas. This openness is the basic philosophy of the uniquely democratic nature of Buddhism.

Sangha members are advised to discuss their affairs, observances, moral practices, meditative development, and teachings. Throughout the Vinaya texts, the Buddha exhorted his disciples to assemble and decide matters according to the majority's viewpoint. The Sangha has a very systematic and democratic nature due to the fact that in the Sangha, all members have equal rights and opportunities to determine and administer affairs. Furthermore, decentralization of power is as important as the distribution of products. The power of this system depends on all members. In the process of determining things, everyone's consent is sought and the majority vote is respected. The Sangha incorporates the idea of the absentee vote (chandaṁ hara) for the ill or disabled monk. The vote would be delivered to the Sangha by a messenger even when no postal system existed. Thus, within Buddhist philosophy, the idea was held that the right to rule a society or a country was based on the consent of the subjects ruled which is basic democracy. Hence,

---

[10]Hermann Oldenberg, ed., The Vinaya Piṭakaṁ (The Mahávagga), Vol. I, pp. 20-21. The quoted passage is translated as, "I, monks, am freed from all snares, both those of devas and those of men. And you, monks, are freed from all snares, both those of devas and those of men:" The Book of the Discipline (Vinaya-Piṭaka) (Mahávagga), Vol. IV, translated by I.B. Horner (London: Luzac & Company, LTD., 1951), p. 28.

the right of self-determination was not ruled out for the sake of the minority's self-interest.

When ordination of a candidate to a position in the Sangha is to take place, rules and regulations must be explained to him before he is actually admitted to the Sangha. However, certain rules should not be explained to a new candidate[11] right away. The main idea here is not to allow the candidate to withdraw his application, but to encourage him to go forward with it. But it must be understood that nobody should be admitted to the Sangha or to any position without his asking. Violation of this rule is an offence of wrong-doing (dukkata) by those who give an admission. The applicant has to approach the assembled Sangha in a humble manner, salute it and request the position sought by saying: "Samghaṁ bhante upasampadaṁ yácámi, ullumpatu maṁ bhante samgho anukampaṁ upádáya."[12] To make sure that he really desires the position requested and that he has properly followed procedure, he has to repeat this request three times.

During this procedure, the whole Sangha remains silent. At this stage, one or two of the Sangha members who are experienced and competent inform the Sangha by saying, "Honored Sirs, let the Sangha hear what I am saying. This man desires ordination as a monk (bhikkhu) from so and so venerable sir. This candidate requests the Sangha to ordain him through the preceptor (upajjháya).[13]

---

[11]The Book of the Discipline (Mahávagga), Vol. IV, translated by I.B. Horner, 76.

[12]"Honored Sirs, I request the Sangha for ordination; may the Sangha raise me up to the position out of compassion." Hermann Oldenberg, ed., The Vinaya Piṭakaṁ (The Mahávagga), Vol. I, p. 57.

[13]The upajjháya must be a very qualified person to supervise the behavior of the pupil. He must have been well trained by his preceptor for a period of at least five years. Morally, he must be perfect, intelligent and experienced. Usually, he has continuously been a monk for ten or more years. An unintelligent person has no right to ordain another monk even if he has been a monk for many years. The duration of experience and intelligence are equally important factors. If after ordination has been given to a new candidate the preceptor dies or leaves his position for a certain reason another qualified monk must be chosen as soon as possible to supervise the newly ordained monk (navaka bhikkhu) so that he can

If it seems all right to the Sangha, I will interview the candidate about stumbling-blocks." If every member keeps silent then the announcer, by observing that fact, makes an affirmative decision on the application, by saying "This is the motion"[14] set forth here.

After obtaining consent from the whole Sangha, the stumbling-blocks (antaráyike dhamme) will be reviewed separately by one or two of the competent representatives of the Sangha. The following questions are asked by the Sangha representatives,

> Santi te evarúpá ábádhá kuttham gando kiláso soso apamáro, manusso'si, puriso'si, bhujisso'si, anano'si, na'si rájabhato, anuññáto'si mátápitúhi, paripunnavïsativasso'si, paripunnan te pattacïvaram, kimnámo'si, konámo te upajjháyo`ti.[15]

---

improve himself in the good laws (dhamma) and discipline (vinaya). Usually such a replacement is arranged with the mutual understanding of the monk who needs a spiritual advisor and the abbot of his temple, or other authoritative fellow monks who know his situation. In any event, the pupil has to make a formal request for the replacement of his preceptor. Therefore, he should approach a senior authoritative monk in the humble manner (as shown in Confession and Amendment section) and formally request that he be his master or spiritual advisor. Because of the pre-arrangement of this program the senior monk gives his consent to be the master which includes the undertaking of all necessary responsibility incurred therein.

[14]The process of a formal proposal in a deliberative assembly of the Sangha and the resolution is known by the word "motion (ñatti)."

[15]"Do you have diseases like: leprosy, ulceration, eczema, consumption, or epilepsy? Are you a human being? Are you a man? Are you a free man? Are you without debts? Are you in the royal (governmental) service? Do you have your parents' permission? Are you full twenty years of age? Are you complete as to bowl and robes? What is your name? What is your preceptor's name?" The Vinaya Pitakam (The Mahávagga), Vol. I, p. 93.

41

Then the Sangha will be informed by the questioning monks. These monks say,

> Sunátu me bhante saṁgho. ayam itthannámo itthannámassa áyasmato upasampadápekkho. itthannámo samghaṁ upasampadaṁ yácati itthannámena upajjháyena. yadi saṁghassa pattakallaṁ, saṁgho itthannámaṁ upasampádeyya itthannámena upajjháyena. esá ñatti... Saṁgho itthannámaṁ upasampádeti itthannámena upajjháyena. yassáyasmato khamati itthannámassa upasampadá itthannámena upajjhyáyena, so tunh'assa, yassa nakkhamati, so bháseyya. dutiyampi ... tatiyampi etaṁ atthaṁ vadámi _ la _ upasampanno saṁghena itthannámo itthannámena upajjháyena. khamati samghassa, tasmá tunhï, evaṁ etaṁ dhárayámïti.[16]

---

[16]This (Páli) ordination procedure can be described in the following way: "Venerable Sirs, let the Sangha listen to me. This person desires ordination from the so and so venerable preceptor. He is quite pure in regard to the stumbling blocks and he is complete as to bowl and robes. This person is requesting the Sangha for ordination under the so and so preceptor. If it seems all right to the Sangha, let the Sangha ordain so and so person under the preceptor ... The Sangha is ordaining so and so person under so and so preceptor. If the ordination of this person under this preceptor is pleasing to the Venerable ones, let them keep silent, to whomever it is not pleasing let him speak out ..." As usual, this is repeated three times. If all the members of the Sangha keep silent the candidate is regarded as ordained by the Sangha through the preceptor. Then the announcer ends his information by affirmatively saying, "It is pleasing to the Sangha, therefore, every member of the Sangha keeps silent. Thus, I understand this ordination is completed." The Vinaya Pitakaṁ (The Mahávagga), Vol. I, p. 57. See also The Book of the Discipline (Mahávagga), translated by I.B. Horner, pp. 73-74; and Ibid., p. 123.

The procedure for the appointment of officials to any position is very similar. In the early tradition, the preceptor (upajjhāya) was chosen within the group of monks gathered in the boundary (sīmā) hall. Later on, as the Sangha functioning became more political, any position in the group was determined outside the Sangha assembly in sīmā. To maintain the tradition, ceremonial selection was made again within the sīmā. The selection of a position in the Sangha can be closely likened to the election of any modern political leader.

All members of the Sangha have to agree on the informal selection. Then the formal selection is made in the Sīmā. This is a good example of the democratic nature of the Sangha which has an institutional and social administration built within it. Agreement is to be vested in the whole Sangha. Similarly, when we apply this religious ethical principle to an administrative charter, or a governmental system, everyone theoretically has equal opportunity to express his opinion on important decisions in a given society, or country. In addition, such a system supposedly increases the opportunity to nominate and elect the best candidates.

The Buddha allowed monks to inform candidates of these ordination rules ahead of time. This allowed the candidates time to think clearly about whether they were facing stumbling-blocks or not. The candidates must be very honest and the monks must question them carefully. Their questioning is similar to an employer's reviewing applications for jobs today. One single mistake in the review can jeopardize the process of dealing with the actual facts and can also affect the admission of newcomers.

In terms of building a monastery, or even a hut, the Sangha must obtain general agreement from the required quorum of members. For this purpose, monks must be brought together to inspect and mark off the appropriate site. The following passage shows that a monk who wants to build a hut, after clearing a site, must respectfully make a request of the Sangha by saying, "ahaṁ bhante samyācikāya kutiṁ kattukāmo assāmikaṁ attuddesam, so'haṁ bhante samghaṁ kuṭivatthuolokanaṁ yācāmīti."[17] This request is to be repeated three times.

---

[17]"Venerable sirs, begging in company for my own advantage, I wish to build a hut. It has no benefactor. I request the Sangha for an inspection of the site for a hut." Hermann Oldenberg, ed., The Vinaya Piṭakaṁ (The Suttavibhanga) (First

After the request, if it is possible, the entire Sangha would inspect the site for the hermitage. If the whole Sangha is not able to do so, then it must select experienced monks who know how to perform the duties involved. They must decide which area has an open space around it. They must know which site fulfills all the requirements for the purpose and which does not. To select the representative monks, the Sangha follows democratic procedures which are analogous to that of the ordination procedure. The Sangha must be informed by a competent monk.

This passage explains that the monk makes a request by saying,

> sunátu me bhante samgho. ayam itthannámo
> bhikkhu samyácikáya kuṭim kattukámo assámikam
> attuddesam, so samgham kuṭivatthuolokanam yácati.
> yadi samghassa pattakallam, samgho itthannámañ ca
> itthannámañ ca bhikkhú sammanneyya
> itthannámassa bhikkhuno kuṭivatthum oloketum.
> esá ñatti. sunátu me bhante samgho. ayam
> itthannámo bhikkhu ... yácati. samgho itthannamañ
> ca itthannámañ ca bhikkhú sammannati
> itthannámassa bhikkhuno kuṭivatthum oloketum.
> yassáyasmato khamati itthannámassa ca
> itthannámassa ca bhikkhúnam sammuti
> itthanámassa bhikkhuno kuṭivatthum oloketum so
> tunh'assa, yassa na kkkhamati so bháseyya.
> sammatá samghena ittahannámo ca itthannámo ca
> bhikkhú itthannámassa bhikkhuno kuṭivatthum
> oloketum. khamati samghassa tasmá tunhï, evam
> etam dhárayámïti.[18]

Part), Vol. III (London: Published for the Páli Text Society by Luzac & Company, LTD., 1964), p. 149.

[18]"Venerable sirs, let the Sangha listen to what I say. Such and such a monk, requesting in our company, for his own advantage, desires to build a monastery which has no other benefactor (besides himself). He requests the Sangha for an inspection of the site. If the time is right for the Sangha to make an inspection it should appoint (such and such) monks to inspect the site. If it seems all right to

These representatives of the Sangha, having inspected the site, decide whether that spot is fit for a monastery or not. If it does not meet the requirements, they object to it, or if it is all right, then they inform the Sangha about it. But before approval can be given to begin building, the required quorum of members must establish the boundary (sīmā). A ceremonial process is required for which the individual monk must approach the Sangha again and beg for the site. At this stage the Sangha usually accepts it. In a similar fashion, Dabbamalla was elected (conferred) by the Sangha to the position of Senāsanagāhāpaka and Bhattuddesaka to distribute room and board to the Sangha members.[19]

This is the democratic system we find in ancient Buddhist scripture that can easily be used by the present parliamentary or governmental systems. By democratic system, I mean to say the system of governing which listens to the voice of the majority, and takes into account public opinion. Under the democratic system everybody has the equal right and authority to express his ideas on how to manage the governing system (body) and to share the results thereof. There is no bias towards or prejudiced treatment of anyone in this society.

What happens when a particular member of the Sangha does not like a certain candidate for personal or whatever reasons? He must give a sufficient reason for his feelings to the Sangha. Otherwise, he will be reprimanded or given a demerit by the Sangha for his bias. But if he really has good reason, his veto or objection will be taken into consideration by the Sangha. Such a case will be decided by the majority. The objective consideration of each case is the purpose of this system which is governed by disciplinary rules and regulations.

---

the venerable sirs to depute the inspection of a site for a monastery to such and such monks for that monk, please be silent; if it is not then you should speak out." As usual, this motion is repeated three times. If all the members of the Sangha keep silent then the announcer ends his proposal by emphatically saying, "These monks are deputed by the Sangha to inspect the site for a monastery for such and such a monk. It seems all right to the Sangha, therefore, they are silent. Thus I understand it." Hermann Oldenberg, ed., The Vinaya Piṭakaṁ (The Suttavibhanga), Vol. III, p. 150.

[19]Hermann Oldenberg, ed., The Vinaya Piṭakaṁ (The Mahāvagga), Vol. I, pp. 272-273.

In the Sangha every member has equal rights with regard to practicing the disciplines, the ethical codes, and expressing and exchanging views or ideas. Equal rights are held in making decisions, rendering mutual help concerning daily affairs and attending to the observance of moral conduct and the like. The Buddha advised his Sangha that every member should treat the other as his brother. They should meet one another from time to time and share their material and spiritual gains.

The Disciplinary Rules and Regulations

As mentioned in the Introduction, in general, the Buddha expounded "dhamma"[20] to all kinds of people. But disciplinary rule (vinaya) were normally preached exclusively only for monks, very few for novices (sámanera). Even though the vinaya are as important for the Sangha as constitutional laws are for the governmental institution (parliament) of a given country, the Buddha often placed dhamma first and vinaya second in relevance to his teachings.[21] On the other hand, it is interesting to recall that there is no mention of vinaya in his several orientation-preachings,[22] or developmental stages of the Sangha. Even when vinaya rules were not explicitly mentioned or instructed, many monks and lay people attained the goal of Buddhist practice, arahattahood or nibbána.[23] Only after disorder within the Sangha had arisen did the Buddha lay down the vinaya rules in order to prevent it from happening again. The rules helped to organize and regulate the Sangha more properly and efficiently.

---

[20]The term "dhamma" means "religion." It also carries the meaning of "doctrine" including mental and physical, conceivable and inconceivable phenomenon and is usually meant for all common folk and monks.

[21]Hermann Oldenberg, ed., The Vinaya Pitakam (The Mahávagga), Vol. I, p. X.

[22]The Book of the Discipline (Mahávagga), Vol. Vol. IV, translated by I.B. Horner (London: Luzac & Company, LTD., 1951), p. 13ff; Ibid., p. 45ff.

[23]In fact, it appeared that the more the vinaya rules increased, the fewer the number of people attained arahattahood or nibbána.

Here one can see the crucial differences between the essential purposes, structures, and uses of dhamma and vinaya. Putting more emphasis on the maintenance of the vinaya rules, the Buddha said that as long as the practice of these continued (even though the Abhidhamma-Piṭaka and Sutta-Piṭaka were forgotten) the teaching (sāsana) of the Buddha would still survive in the world; otherwise, it would hardly be possible for the sāsana to survive.[24]

According to the Buddha, discipline (vinaya) is the most important of the three Piṭakas for the survival of sāsana. Moral conduct (sīla) is the core of monastic discipline and is the vitality of Buddhist teachings. Here, the Buddha was again implying that when monks do not practice vinaya, his sāsana is lost. Nothing can make the real doctrine (saddhamma) disappear or make the Sangha decline but the hollow or stupid man (moghapurisa) within it. The Buddha said, "Atha kho idheva te uppajjanti moghapurisā ye imaṁ saddhammaṁ antaradhāpenti."[25] Through this expression one can understand how much more powerful and important the internal policy of a given institution is than that of the external one. Therefore, we can conclude that the significance of dhamma and vinaya are as the different parts of the same whole, existing for different purposes of religious and philosophical life.

Vinaya rules are used for regulating the outward conduct of the individual and the collective practice of the Sangha. Dhamma is for the inward development and the attainment of a good life. In any case, we may say that moral codes are for the welfare of those in monastic life but also include common people. They lead the individual through practice to nibbāna. If there were no proper moral

---

[24]The Book of Discipline (Mahāvagga), Vol. IV, p. 127.

[25]"But here in the Sangha itself foolish men arise, and it is they who make the true laws (saddhamma) disappear." M. Leon Feer, ed., Samyutta-Nikāya, Part II (London: Published for the Pāli Text Society by Messrs. Luzac & Company, LTD., 1960), 224. The Book of the Kindred Sayings (Samyutta-Nikāya), Part II, translated by Mrs. Rhys Davids (London: Published for the Pāli Text Society by Luzac & Company LTD., 1952), p. 152: There are various lowering things that conduce to the obscuration and disappearance of the true teachings (saddhamma). It is when monks and nuns, men and women lay followers live in irreverence and are unruly toward the Buddha, the Dhamma, the Sangha, the training (sikkhā) and concentrative study.

rules and regulations for a community or Sangha, the group would not function well. The same holds true for the lay community. In fact, it would be in a state of confusion.

The great hope is that such provisions, i.e., the rules, would enable the persistent and long lasting propagation of the teachings. Venerable Sáriputta, the chief disciple, had earnestly requested the Buddha to stipulate the course of training and to appoint the pátimokkha (compendium of monastic rules) rules for monks. But the Buddha refused to do it at once, by saying, "ágamehi tvaṁ Sáriputta, ágamehi tvaṁ Sáriputta. tathágato'va tattha kálaṁ jánissati."[26] The Buddha waited. He did not make constitutional laws, or vinaya rules for the Sangha until it was necessary. Only after a monk had committed a sin or an improper act, then did the Buddha lay down a rule counteracting that particular act.

> Abstain from all evil; acquire merit; purify your
> thought.
> Patience is the greatest austerity;
> nibbána is the goal.
> No ascetic, no recluse is he who
> injures, who vexes another!
> Hurt none by word or deed: live
> secluded, and restrained, moderate
> in eating, in resting and sleeping;
> devoted to contemplation.[27]

All Pátimokkha rules evolved out of this. The Pátimokkha has an important position in the history of the disciplinary codes, serving as the basic formula of the entire Vinaya-Piṭaka. It was not an easy task to lay down the disciplinary rules and the Buddha spent much time formulating the Pátimokkha rules and managing his

---

[26]Hermann Oldenberg, ed., The Vinaya Piṭakaṁ (The Suttavibhanga), Vol. III (London: Published for the Páli Text Society by Luzac & Company, LTD., 1964), p. 9. The quoted passage has been translated as, "Wait Sáriputta, wait, Sáriputta. The tathágata will know the right time for that." The Book of the Discipline (Vinaya Piṭaka), Vol. I, translated by I.B. Horner, p. 18.

[27]See The Dhammapada: 14:5-7.

Sangha properly. According to the situation of his Sangha members, the Buddha eventually established 227 disciplinary rules (pátimokkha) (which are applied equally to all Sangha members). His desire was to counteract any negative behavior by a monk if he (the Buddha) considered it to be an impediment to the spiritual path of nibbána. Thus, the Buddha had his own religio-political constitution which is still valid. All vinaya rules are constitutional laws of the Sangha. These rules deal with the entire way of life of the Sangha members and also deal with the relations of the Sangha members to the public, and with other religions. Therefore, the vinaya can be considered as a code of civil and criminal laws, dealing with the Sangha, the laity and other religious ascetics. The vinaya laws are classified into various groups. Certain ones deal with crimes, finance, education, construction and day to day business; others with social etiquette and religious practices. None of these rules makes an exception for the law-maker. This is the oldest democratic system in the world.

In a way, the Pátimokkha rules are similar to any social rules or laws. However, the Pátimokkha is not just a series of rules created for a society, but is based upon a clear moral principle. Moreover, the Buddhist moral code (or the Pátimokkha) is incorporated with the natural law, the law of karma. This tacitly considers even an unwitnessed act, while the social laws deal mainly with what appears on the surface (i.e., a problem currently existing in the world). The acceptance of this natural law is genuine democracy. It makes a person self reliant and considerate. The Pátimokkha rules are systematically based upon the practice of chastity (brahmacariya), moral character and dhamma ideals. They lead the follower to the highest goal of Buddhist practice. The Pátimokkha rules are very instructive and consider the smallest details. These rules are classified in various categories according to their ethical and religious significance. The gravest are first and the least serious last.

The most serious category, literally called "a defeat (párájiká)",[28] consists of four major rules. They prohibit sexual intercourse, stealing, murdering or causing someone to murder another, and falsely claiming to possess supernatural power or being a superman (uttarimanussadhamma). Unlike minor rules, these

---

[28]If a monk violates one of these four rules he is considered to be in "defeat" and therefore, the rule itself is called" a defeat (párájiká)."

major rules are not allowed to be changed or modified. Violation of the same results in the expulsion of the transgressor from the Sangha once and for all.

There are thirteen rules entailing the formal meeting of the Sangha (sanghádisesa). A monk who fails to observe them receives a heavy penalty. The first rule was established against the intentional emission of semen. The other four were warnings about involvement with a female. Two were concerned with the construction of a private hut or dwelling. Another rule dealt with the false accusation of a monk (by another monk) and the intention to defame or expel him from the Sangha. Other rules dealt with the attempt to create a schism in the Sangha, or the indulgence in bad habits. If a monk transgresses one of these Sanghádisesa rules he must undergo a heavy punishment. At least twenty monks must be present in order to facilitate the punishment of the transgressor.[29] Among these thirteen Sanghádisesa, nine are considered broken after one offence and four others are not completely broken until the third admonition.

The third category has two rules concerning situations where there is uncertainty (aniyata). One situation involves a monk with a woman in a secluded place where it is suitable for sexual intercourse to take place. The other concerns a monk and a woman in an open space where they can speak privately or lewdly (i.e., where no one else can hear it although anyone around there can see the monk and the woman talking).

The fourth category comprises thirty nissaggiya pácittiya rules. These rules involve material things which the possessors must forfeit to the Sangha or to another monk. He must carry out their expiation.

The fifth category of pácittiya (the group of rules of expiation) consists of ninety-two rules the transgressor must do the expiation of. The sixth category has seventy-five rules (sikkhápadas) for good manners. If a monk behaves otherwise he must confess the offence of wrong-doing (dukkata). The last seven rules (adhikaranasamatha) deal with legal questions. These disciplinary rules are provided as a solution for settling all sorts of disputes and quarrels within and related to the Sangha.

---

[29]The Book of the Discipline (Vinaya-Pitaka), vol. I, pp. 327-328.

In creating vinaya rules, the Buddha explained their necessity for the following reasons. (1) They promote the beauty and excellence of the Sangha. (2) They increase the ease and well-being of the Sangha. (3) They control undisciplined monks and free the Sangha from the confusion and censure of obstinate persons. (4) They make a comfortable abode for the well-behaved monks. (5) They help restrain evil desires (ásavas) and increase conscientious living and experiencing the present state of dhamma. (6) They thwart the ásavas leading compulsorily to the next world (rebirth). (7) They make life pleasant for those who are unpleasant. (8) They develop a deeper pleasantness for those who are already pleased. (9) They establish and insure the survival of the true dhamma. (10) They support and favor the Vinaya itself.[30] These were the basic aims of the Buddha in laying down the moral codes (vinaya).

The Buddha amended many rules and regulations in order to suit the time and place so that monastic life would run smoothly. He attempted to protect the faith and encourage the generosity of lay followers who supported the Sangha in the hope of obtaining merits. The Buddha prohibited monks from draining the resources of lay people. At the same time, they were not to refuse offers of food, clothing and other things in order that they not hurt the feelings of people who were pursuing piety.

In her introduction to the Vinaya-Piṭaka I.B. Horner correctly understood the importance of keeping the friendship of kings, on whom the success of the Sangha largely depended. Kings set examples for the lay people by their pious acts of giving. Such acts inspired the laity to do the same thing. She made a keen observation about King Pasenadi's device for letting the Buddha know (without speaking to him directly) that arahanta monks were sporting in the water of the river Aciravati. His queen Mallikā was of the opinion that either there was no rule prohibiting monks from sporting in the water, or that these monks were not aware of it. Apparently, her first instinct was correct.[31] Pasenadi's encounter with the

---

[30]Ibid., pp. 37-38; see also The Book of the Gradual Sayings (Anguttara-Nikáya), Vol. V, translated by F.L. Woodward (London: Published for the Páli Text Society by Luzac & Company, LTD., 1972), p. 50.

[31]The Book of the Discipline(Vinaya-Piṭaka), Vol. II, translated by I.B. Horner, pp. 390-391.

monks by the river bank helped establish pácittiya rule LIII. This rule discouraged monks from sporting in the water.

Monks playfully bathed themselves until dark even though they saw King Bimbisára waiting on the side, inconveniencing himself by his forbearance, to take a bath there. So the Buddha laid down pácittiya rule LVII which prohibited monks from bathing more often than once in two weeks. This proved pernicious to robes and dwelling places. Because in

> the fever weather, at a time of wind and rain, when making repairs or going on a journey, monks lay down to rest with their limbs damp from rain or sweat. And the restriction on bathing was uncomfortable for those who were ill. This is a rule whose various adjustments are the direct outcome of a tropical climate.[32]

At first, the Buddha did not allow monks to store food indoors, or to cook food indoors, but when necessity arose due to a scarcity of food in Vesali, he allowed monks to store and cook food in the house in order to protect it.[33] Later on, when a famine was over and there was plenty to eat, the Buddha again amended the rule. He told them not to make use of food which was stored indoors, cooked indoors, or cooked by themselves. The Buddha revised the pácittiya[34] rule on eating in a group-meal (gaṇabhojana) seven times and seven legalized exceptions were made.

With the forfeiture rule (nissaggiya-pácittiya XXII) the Buddha prohibited monks from asking for a bowl from people. Later, however, when the need arose the Buddha amended the rule by saying, "anujánámi bhikkhave naṭṭhapattassa vá

---

[32]The Book of the Discipline (Vinaya Piṭaka), Vol. II, translated by I.B. Horner, p. XXVIII.

[33]Ibid., pp. 287-289.

[34]Ibid., p. 326.

bhinnapattassa vá pattam viññápetun ti."[35] The Buddha continued to specify and amend the rule several times.

To the rule on paramparábhojana (Pácittiya XXXIII) or eating meals out of turn, four exceptions were permitted. In pácittiya rule LVII six exceptions are allowed for the rule that a monk should not take a bath at intervals of less than half a month.[36]

Amendment of another rule occurred when monks slept. When monks carelessly exposed their bodies, mumbled and snored in the presence of lay-followers, criticism came upon them. To prevent this situation the Buddha established the rule prohibiting a monk from lying down in sleeping-quarters with one who is not fully ordained an upasampadá bhikkhu. But because of this rule Ráhula, the only son of the Buddha (Siddhattha), on one occasion had to lie down in a privy (latrine in India) and spend the night there. The Buddha amended this rule, so that monks were allowed to sleep in quarters with one who was not fully ordained for only two or three nights.[37]

He amended rules about using sandals also. The Buddha amended many other rules as well. The Buddha was quite aware of the necessity to amend laws when on his death bed said, "Äkankhamáno ánanda sangho accayena khuddánukkhuddakáni sikkhápadáni samúhantu."[38] Hence almost no law or rule

---

[35]"Monks! I allow you, whose bowl is destroyed or whose bowl is broken, to ask for a bowl." Hermann Oldenberg, ed., The Vinaya Pitaka (The Suttavibhanga), Vol. III (London: Published for the Páli Text Society by Luzac & Company, LTD., 1964), p. 245.

[36]The Book of the Discipline (Vinaya Pitaka), translated by I.B. Horner, p. XXVII.

[37]Ibid., Vol. II, pp. 194-196.

[38]"After my passing away, Änanda, if the Sangha so wishes it can abolish lesser and minor precepts (disciplinary rules and regulations)": T.W. Rhys Davids and J Estlin Carpenter, eds., The Dïgha-Nikáya, Vol. II (London: Geoffrey Cumberlege, Oxford University Press, 1947), p. 154.

is perfect and eternal in the world. It may need to be amended and improved according to the time and situation.

Bearing the advantages of morality in mind, the Buddha advised the Sangha to learn and recite by heart the entire collection of Pátimokkha rules. The memorization of the Pátimokkha rules is as important as the duty of citizens to know basic laws of their country. This recitation was to be performed every fortnight so that monks might not forget them. Accordingly, after purifying their moral conscience by confession, all members assembled and a competent monk recited the entire text. The recitation of the rules is still essential for the Sangha.

Every member dwelling at a particular area or place attends the recitation. If less than four bhikkhus are present the Pátimokkha recitation is invalid. Before joining the recitation ceremony, all the bhikkhus must confess offenses (ápatti) committed against any of the established rules.

If a member has committed one of the four párájikás he will be expelled from the Sangha at once. One who has committed one of the thirteen sanghádisesas will be given a heavy punishment called a parivása. A confession will be required of any who has committed other minor offenses and he will be free from them. Those having committed no offence at all are declared to be morally pure. When all have had moral purification, the Pátimokkha recitation commences immediately.

This procedure itself is one of the specialties in the Pátimokkha rules (codes). This is the exercise of good moral character of the Sangha. The recital of the Pátimokkha text in brief is allowed only when there is danger to life or celibacy (brahmacariya).[39] The Pátimokkha should not be recited, as Devadatta performed it, before an assembly that contained lay persons.[40] Nor should it be recited on a daily[41] basis. The recital of the Pátimokkha text is a serious matter.

---

[39]The Book of the Discipline (Mahávagga), translated by I.B. Horner, p. 148: The dangers mentioned here include danger from kings, danger from thieves, fire, water, human and non-human beings, beasts of prey, creeping things and so on.

[40]Ibid., p. 152 & p. 180.

[41]Ibid., pp. 131-132.

Only an authorized and competent monk should recite the Pátimokkha text at the proper time.

A monk qualified to recite the Pátimokkha must be very wise. He must be an expert on law (dhamma) and on the disciplinary rules and regulations (vinaya). He must know the summaries. He must be keenly aware of the traditions (ágatágamo) handed down. He must be experienced, clever, conscientious, scrupulous and desirous of training. Such a monk is not only qualified to recite the Pátimokkha, but should also be extended special courtesies (sangahetabbo) by other monks. He should be given (anuggahetabbo) clay (soap), tooth-wood (tooth-brush), or water for washing his face.[42] This monk should be encouraged and supported by his fellow monks.

The legitimate process of the Pátimokkha recital (which is part of the whole text itself) is made by the reciter as follows:

> sunátu me bhante saṁgho. ajj'uposatho pannaraso.
> yadi saṁghassa pattakallaṁ, saṁgho uposathaṁ
> kareyya pátimokkhaṁ uddiseyya. kiṁ saṁghassa
> pubbakiccaṁ párisuddhiṁ áyasmanto árocetha.
> pátimokkhaṁ uddisissámi, taṁ sabbeva santá
> sádhukaṁ suṇoma manasikaroma. yassa siyá ápatti,
> so ávikareyya, asantiyá ápattiyá tunhï
> bhávitabbaṁ, tunhïbhávena kho panáyasmante
> parisuddhá'ti vedissámi. yathá kho pana
> paccekaputthassa veyyákaranaṁ hoti, evaṁ eva
> evarúpáya parisáya yávatatiyaṁ anussavitam hoti.
> yo pana bhikkhu yávatatiyaṁ anussaviyamáne
> saramáno santiṁ ápattiṁ návikareyya,
> sampajánamusávád'assa hoti. sampajánamusávádo
> kho panáyasmanto antaráyiko dhammo vutto
> bhagavatá. tasmá saramánena bhikkhúná ápannena

---

[42]Ibid., p. 157.

visuddhápekkhena santï ápatti ávikátabbá ávikatá hi'ssa phásu hotïti.[43]

He recites the entire Pátimokkha text. At the conclusion of the recitation, all the Sangha members recite the Metta Sutta, or the discourse on loving-kindness, together. Afterwards monks sometimes discuss dhamma and vinaya.

Pátimokkha rules are observed conscientiously and voluntarily as opposed to the practice of governmental laws which are enforced by the use of external forces or punishment. As in any government body, in the Sangha moral codes are demanded. If there are no such disciplinary rules, or monks fail to follow them, then there is no peace in the Sangha. It would hardly be possible to bring people into brotherhood. The Buddha laid down the moral rules in order to make his Sangha members equal and to let people live harmoniously and happily while they are here on earth. His basic moral codes, (i.e., not killing, stealing, committing sexual misbehavior, lying and using intoxicants), directly and equally apply to all his followers. These are the fundamentals of the 227 Pátimokkha rules and the whole Vinaya texts. These rules govern all the activities and formal acts within the

----

[43]"Venerable sirs, let the Sangha listen to me. Today is the fifteenth or Observance (uposatha) day. If it seems all right to the Sangha, the Sangha may perform Observance and may recite the Pátimokkha. What is the first duty of the Sangha? Let the venerable sirs announce all purity. I will recite the Pátimokkha while everyone is present, properly listen and pay attention to it. He who may have an offence should tell it. If you have no offence you should be silent. By keeping silent I shall thus understand that the venerable sirs are quite pure. Since there is an answer for each question (paccekaputthassa), this procedure is repeated upto the three times in an assembly like this. Any monk who remembers the existence of an offence while the rules are being announced and fails to reveal it is considered to be deliberately lying. Now venerable sirs, deliberate lying is a thing called a stumbling block (antaráyiko dhammo) by the Buddha. Therefore, the existence of an offence ought to be revealed by a monk who remembers that he has committed the offence and who desires purity; because when it is revealed he receives comfort." Hermann Oldenberg, ed., The Vinaya Piṭakaṁ (The Mahávagga), Vol. I (London: Published for the Páli Text Society by Luzac & Company, LTD., 1964), pp. 102-103.

56

Sangha. One of these rules requires the Sangha members to practice celibacy. Let us consider how they practice it.

Exploring Celibacy in the Buddhist Sangha[44]

Celibacy is considered as holy and good, and its practice occupies a central place, within the Buddhist Sangha (monastic community). People in Buddhist countries do not ask why monks practice celibacy, nor do those practitioners ask why they have to practice it. Without question they accept the tradition of religious celibacy and they either practice it or they do not. Consequently, to the present day, neither the philosophy nor the phenomenon of celibacy has been described in detail.

As Buddhism spreads in Europe and North America, the Buddhist practice of celibacy is being critically questioned for the first time. In those places, many people consider the voluntary abstention from sexual activity strange or even unnatural. Others raise a multitude of questions which express a broad range of concerns, from the purely practical to the spiritual.

For instance, if celibacy were accepted as the ideal of that which is good and holy for everyone, what would be the impact on future generations of humans? Would not the human race become extinct? Is this an intended goal of Buddhist practice?

If celibacy is a Buddhist religious ideal, above and apart from any particular culture's approval of non-celibate priests, what is a student of Buddhism to think of those Japanese and Tibetan priests whose marriages are accepted by their cultures? Are they all subject, by the principle of religion, to ostracism as sinners? If, on the other hand, a culture's approval of active sexual lives for priests changes the applicable religious principle itself, then is not religion merely a convention of the general public and not a revelation of spiritual seers?

---

[44]This article has been submitted for publication in the Middle Way.

This article has been written for the benefit of those who, not having been raised as Buddhists, yet find themselves interested in Buddhist ethics and culture. It elucidates the Buddhist practice of celibacy and its role in the quest for enlightenment.

Buddhist monks are often asked whether they can have sex!
This question is highly ambiguous and may, at any given time, express the questionnaire's doubts as to: (1) whether monks are impotent or physically too weak to function sexually; (2) whether they are mentally dull and have no interest in sexual indulgence; (3) whether their sexual organs are ritually cut away; (4) whether they are allowed by the authority of the religion to practice sexual intercourse; (5) whether monks can financially afford to have wives/girlfriends; (6) whether they can afford time to become involved in sexual practice etc..

Answering to this ambiguous question, one can say that (1) monks are not impotent nor physically too weak to function sexually; (2) they are not dull either and may have an interest in sexual indulgence, but they are willing to control it; (3) their sexual organs are intact and it has never been a Buddhist ritual to sexually mutilate monks so as to make sexual intercourse impossible for them; (4) the major concern for this practice is that monks are not allowed by the authority of the religion to practice sexual intercourse; (5) financially monks have to admit their state of poverty but because money is not everything in reality, the low financial status does not block sexual affairs if they wish to do so; (6) they may not have time to fool around, however, this is not the absolute factor to block the sexuality. Hence, where there is will there is a way. This way for monks, however, is the middle path, leading to nirvana.

Associated with asceticism, ascetics practiced celibacy in Asia. History shows that the practice of celibacy is as old as asceticism in India, much older than the historical Buddha himself. Before the Buddha was born, there were ascetics who practiced celibacy as a spiritual discipline conducive to the attainment of salvation.

Although celibacy was quite common, the practice may not have been very strict since some rishis or ascetics took their wives with them to practice asceticism in solitary places in India. According to commentarial literature, some of them were said to have had progeny or offspring. For example, Dukulaka and Parika, who did not consummate their marriage, became ascetics. It is written, however, that later on conception took place when Dukulaka touched Parika's navel with his finger at the proper time.[45] When their son was born they called him Sama (also known as Suvannasama, meaning golden Sama).

Another source tells of a young married couple, Pippali and Bhadda Kapilani, both of whom were excellent in health and beauty. It is said that they did not consummate their marriage, but spent the night separated by a garland of flowers.[46] They placed the flowers between them to test their sexual discipline. The flowers did not wither away, nor were the blossoms crushed by them, because their sexual desire did not arise. Later, both of them left household life. Thus, it seems that the exact nature of the practice of celibacy was left to the individual's choice.

When the Buddha prescribed and commended the practice of celibacy, over 2500 years ago, Buddhism co-existed in India with Hinduism and Jainism. The practice of celibacy was common to all three religious traditions. As these religions became more formalized and the public became more aware of them, the strictness with which their disciples practiced celibacy became a matter of competition -- both among monks of the same religion and between the different religious communities. Celibacy came to be held in the highest regard for its own sake, as well as for the pleasing impression it created in pious lay people. Once the strict practice of celibacy had become such a strong norm, its transgression came to be seen as equivalent to a crime like murder or robbery in these religious communities. A violator of the rule was permanently ostracized as a sinful person.

One of the Buddha's major concerns for his disciples' moral lives was with their commitment to and contentment with celibacy. An abundance of references to these topics can be found scattered throughout ancient Buddhist texts. In his first sermon the Buddha mentioned sexual intercourse as a base or low act performed by common people (as opposed to monks). He said that addiction to attractive sense-pleasures and addiction to self-torment or self-mortification are both extremes. The Buddha counseled his ordained disciples against both of these

---

[45]G.P. Malalasekera, Dictionary of Pali Proper Names, Vol. II (London: Published for The Pali Text Society by Luzac & Company, LTD., 1960), p. 1097f.

[46]G.P. Malalasekera, Dictionary of Pali Proper Names, Vol. II, p. 476f.

practices since, as extremes, they are inconsistent with the middle path that leads to nirvana.[47]

In The Anguttara Nikaya, the Buddha explicitly explained sexual attraction as the strongest biological and psychological urge in both men and women. Their sight, sound, touch, and smell mutually attract each other's heart. The Buddha himself admitted that he had not seen or known any other attractions stronger or more attractive than man's appearance, touch, sound, etc. to a woman and woman's to a man.[48] This gravity of attraction pulls them one towards the other, by the medium of sight or appearance, sound, touch and even imagination.

Women were depicted as dangerous for men's celibacy and men for women's. And yet in the time of the Buddha, some ordained men and women were found to be fondling one another and practicing sexual intercourse.[49] The sexual urge, which is hard to control in both men and women, was exhibited in the practice of ordained disciples, transgressing moral precepts laid down by the Buddha.

As a consequence, the Buddha had to act decisively, rigidly refining, reiterating, and re-enforcing the moral code numerous times. He had to prohibit every kind of sexual behavior by members of the Sangha (monastic community) as unfit acts. He totally and flatly banned all forms of sexual practices. After the formation and declaration of the Buddha's moral code prohibiting sexual intercourse, those monks or nuns who performed one or more of the three sexual acts (namely heterosexual, oral, and anal sexual practices) were permanently ostracized from his Sangha community. The Buddha punished the transgression of chastity-rule in the same manner as crimes like robbery and murder.[50]

---

[47]The Book of the Discipline (Vinaya-Piṭaka) (Mahavagga) Vol. IV, translated by I.B. Horner (London: Luzac & Company ITD., 1962), p. 15.

[48]Bhikkhu J. Kashyap, gen. ed., The Anguttara Nikaya (Ekakanipata, Dukanipata & Tikanipata), Vol. I (Bihar: Pali Publication Board, 1960), pp. 3-4.

[49]See Bhikkhu Parajika I and Bhikkhuni Parajika I.

[50]The Book of the Discipline (Vinaya-Piṭaka) (Suttavibhanga), Vol. I, translated by I.B. Horner (London: Published for The Pali Text Society by Luzac & Company, LTD., 1949), p. 40; also compare Parajika I-IV.

Those priests who practiced masturbation, or intentionally emitted semen by some means, were punished by the formal meeting of the Sangha. The Buddha said, "Intentional emission of semen except during a dream is an offence requiring a formal meeting of the Order."[51]

Monks who violated the celibacy rule by performing masturbation were placed on probation. During the probationary period, they were prohibited from preaching and carrying on any other formal communal religious activities such as participating in Patimokkha recitation, in formal meeting of the Sangha, and ordaining other people into the religion.

Before the Buddha's passing away one of the main concerns of his close attendant monk, Ananda, was how to deal with a female. He entreated the Buddha, ""How are we to conduct ourselves, lord, with regard to womankind?"" The Buddha responded him saying not to look at her; if you (Ananda) happen to look at womankind, do not talk to her. The Buddha said that if you have to look at a woman and talk to her you should guard your mind.[52]

The Buddha said that the moment when one thinks lustfully of a woman one's celibacy becomes imperfect. Thus, in the strictest sense, just thinking of or looking at or touching a woman by a monk may lessen the purity of his celibacy. Despite the apparent rigor of this rule, the Buddhist notion of imperfect or impure celibacy implicitly defines a range of conduct in which the practitioner who falls somewhat short of the ideal can still be considered celibate, although imperfectly so. This practitioner's lapses, if not too serious, would mainly serve to indicate his need to make greater efforts to purify himself.

A vivid illustration of the range of lapses which are subsumed within celibacy can be found in Dhamma Vibhaga Numerical sayings of Dhamma. The paraphrase of it is presented below as follows:

---

[51]The Book of the Discipline (Vinaya-Piṭaka) (Suttavibhanga), Vol. I, translated by I.B. Horner, p. 196.

[52]Dialogues of the Buddha (The Digha Nikaya), Part II, translated by T.W. and C.A.F. Rhys David (London: Published for The Pali Text Society by Luzac & Company, LTD., 1959), p. 154.

There are some monks or recluses who, despite their practice of celibacy, their never having any sexual act with a female, still take pleasure, enjoy themselves and are absorbed in some of the following seven practices, which are called shades of sensuality (sexuality):

1. Taking delight in their being fondled, nursed, bathed and massaged by females; being absorbed in such acts.

2. Taking delight in giggling and exchanging jokes with females; being absorbed thereby.

3. Taking delight in gazing at females' eyes; being absorbed thereby.

4. Taking delight in hearing the voices of females speaking, singing, laughing or crying, outside the walls (of their rooms); being absorbed thereby.

5. Taking delight in recalling what and when they used to speak and laugh with females; being absorbed thereby.

6. Taking delight in seeing laymen, young and old, who enjoy themselves with sensual pleasures; being absorbed thereby.

7. Taking delight in observing the vow of chastity with a view to being born as celestial beings, and are absorbed thereby.

The chaste life of such a monk or recluse is sure to be cut short, cut through, defiled, blemished. His chastity being stained and overridden by these shades of sensuality, he has no hope to free himself from suffering.[53]

What was true during the life of historical Buddha is no less true today. Insofar as their physical capacity for sexual expression is concerned, the monks and nuns of the Buddhist Sangha are no different than the lay persons among whom they live. On the psychological plane, they may naturally experience the pull of

---

[53]H.R.H. the late Supreme Patriarch Prince Vajirananavarorasa, <u>Dhamma Vibhaga Numerical Sayings of Dhamma</u>, Part Two (Bangkok: Mahamakut Rajavidyalaya Press, 2518/1975), pp. 109-110.

sexual attraction to the same degree as other persons and, despite their vows to the contrary, some of them sometimes succumb to that attraction. The Buddhist ascetic must, with understanding, rely on his or her internal self-discipline for the maintenance of the celibate life.

Even monks can imagine what the sexual life would be. Some of them can relate their former experience. But because the religion says that the sexual imagination itself is unwholesome, monks would hardly admit their imaginary world to other people. The thought is not only unwholesome but it is also considered shameful to confess sexual desire to somebody else in the religious community. One who expresses it anyway will only be looked down upon by one's fellows and acquaintances.

But how can monks control their natural biological and psychological urges? When a person sees or believes that there is a great benefit to be gained by in giving up a lesser pleasure or goodness, he can really do it, even if he has to undergo certain aches and pains. Similarly, the Buddha's disciples, who sincerely believe that there is a superior advantage in being celibate, can give up sexual pleasures, even though they have to confront great disturbances. Celibacy is practiced in the hope of attaining greater happiness, or benefit.

When we are very much involved with study, work, or some other absorbing activity, our lustful thoughts are latent and are unable to disturb us. Lustful thoughts disturb us only when we are not occupied with other, stronger objectives or desires. From such experiences we can tell that our sexuality is not merely a matter of physical urges, but also depends greatly on psychological phenomena. Therefore, it is quite possible for a man, by changing his lustful attitude towards a woman, to control his passion. Similarly, a woman can change her thoughts towards a man and thereby control her sexual desire.

If a person often thinks favorably of the opposite sex, sexual desires are more likely to arise in him. It will be harder to control those disturbing desires because he values them highly as pleasurable and good. If, however, he neither thinks favorably of the opposite sex nor sees advantages in sexual involvement, his sexual desires are less active and disturb him less. When he does not place much value on his sexual desires, he can control them instead of them controlling him.

One method used by monks to reduce the sexual appeal of women is to regard all females as close relatives, i.e, their mother, sister, or aunt. Sexual behavior between persons in close family relation is prohibited by law and by custom. For those persons who have internalized this legal and cultural taboo, the practice of celibacy is made easier by imagining that persons of the opposite sex are close relatives. This thinking will inhibit these practitioners to some extent from advancing towards those others because we normally have no lustful thoughts or craving for our relatives. We look at them with a different perspective, with a detached sort of affection rather than with passionate love.

According to tradition, to control sexual desires a monk has to follow, with understanding, the Buddha's teachings on the foulness of human body: underneath the skin all is dirty. According to a Commentary, when he was offered a beautiful woman to wife, the Buddha said:

Having seen Craving, Discontent, and Lust,
I had no desire for the pleasures of love.
What is this body, filled with urine and dung?
I should not be willing to touch it, even with my foot.[54]

This realization applied not only the female; the monk should penetrate and understand fully the reality of his own human body. He should comprehend not only the skin deep appearance of beauty, but also the realities that lie inside the skin. When he considers that inside the skin the human body is full of substances commonly considered filthy (i.e., faeces, urine, pus, saliva, blood, etc.) his thoughts may shrink from indulgence with it. If he repeatedly does this task, his thinking about the physical body will begin to habitually move towards an attitude of avoidance. This avoidance can help the monk's thoughts to become stronger and more sublime. In the sublime state of mind, he is able to comprehend the reality of the world and eventually of nirvana. But controlling sexual desire by this or any other method is neither fun nor easy.

---

[54]Buddhist Legend, Part 3, translated from the original Pali text of the dhammapada Commentary by Eugene Watson Burlingame (London: Published for The Pali Text Society by Luzac & Company, LTD., 1969), pp. 34-35.

One of the psychological factors supporting sexual abstinence is fear. This fear comes in many varieties. They include the fear of being punished by law of karma, by the religious community, by society and in the hereafter. Like shame (hiri) at doing certain things tabooed by society, or religion, fear (ottappa) of the consequences of such actions is regarded as an inner guard of righteousness in the world.[55]

In the religious community, the view is that celibacy is holy (sacred) and sexuality profane. But why? And how? Is sexuality considered unholy (profane) just because the religious authority said so? Or is it intrinsically unholy?

According to Buddhist philosophy, a happiness is attained when sexual desire (excitement) arises in a person and happiness (peace) is also attained when sexual desire is non-existent or does not occur. The sexual pleasure, according to some people, is a kind of food (phassa āhara) which nourishes or vitalizes life. There is no reason why one cannot have sex unless one believes in a particular kind of teaching. But sexual intercourse may be considered futile in the sense that it provides no permanent satisfaction. Before a man has an ejaculation he is dissatisfied because he has not yet experienced orgasm which is the primary goal of the act. But as soon as he has ejaculated he may become indifferent to sex or even perceive it as meaningless. Only for a few seconds does he experience actual pleasure.

In the Brahmajala Sutta, the Buddha condemned the notion that sexual pleasure or sense pleasure is the same as transcendental bliss, the highest nirvana (ditthadhamma nibbana).[56] But a later developed school of Buddhism, Tantric Buddhism, explicitly incorporated sexual pleasure with transcendental bliss.[57] According to Ch'en, "From the concept of the female

[55]Somdet Phra Maha Samana Chao Krom Phraya Vajirananavarorasa, compiled, Navakovada Instructions for newly Ordained Bhikkhus and Samaneras (Bangkok: Maha Makuta Buddhist University, 1971/2514), p. 36.

[56]Dialogues of the Buddha (Digha-Nikaya), Part I, translated by T.W. Rhys David (London: Published by The Pali Text Society, 1973), pp. 49-50.

[57]Herbert V. Guenther, The Tantric View of Life (Berkeley: Shambala Publications Inc., 1972), p. 59 & op. cit.

consorts [of the bodhisattvas] [the] Tantric School draws its idea [is] that nirvana resides in the female organ. Union with the [female] consort results in nirvana or the great bliss."[58] This view breaks with the ideal of traditional Buddhist practice and belief. Traditional Buddhist views tantra as a joke. It may be true that there is hardly any higher pleasure that a worldly man can think of than that of a sexual pleasure (orgasm). In the true sense, however, transcendental bliss (nirvana) cannot be compared with sexual pleasure.

Lay people are not obliged to practice celibacy, nor are they obliged to donate a certain percentage of their income to Buddhist temples. They are permitted to marry. However, strictly professed lay Buddhists take eight precepts once or twice a month on Buddhist holy (uposatha) day. One of these eight precepts is celibacy. Undertaking the precept makes lay people feel great. It is a big deal for them to practice monks like celibacy or continence during one holy day -- a holiday from sexuality.

If willingly practiced, religious celibacy is considered holy or sacred, medically it is healthy, socially it preserves freedom, and economically it is less burdensome. The Buddha said, "From love springs sorrow, from love springs fear; for him who is completely free from love there is no sorrow, whence fear?"[59]

Monks must be celibate their whole lives. Only monks sacrifice -- must sacrifice -- the relish of earthly life in the hope of nirvanic bliss. Some monks choose the chaste way of life voluntarily, but there are others who take monk's ordination for other purposes and are then required to practice celibacy. For the latter, the unwilling practice of celibacy may prove unhealthy.

It is said that such a monk was Seyyasaka. An ordained monk, bhikkhu Seyyasaka was unhappy and frustrated with his celibacy practice. So, he masturbated and in that way he became content, satisfied, and happy. The practice

---

[58]Kenneth K.S. Ch'en, Buddhism In China A Historical Survey (New Jersey: Princeton University Press, 1973), p. 330.

[59]Dhammapada (Text and Translation) by Venerable Acharya Buddharakkhita Thera (Bangalore: Buddha Vacana Trust, Maha Bodhi Society, 1966/2510), 16:5.

of masturbation made him healthy, and good looking too.[60]   Nevertheless, masturbation is prohibited to monks by the Buddha. According to him, a monk becomes ill because he is without virtue or does not practice celibacy (abrahma-cariya).[61] This, he said, is one of the causes of illnesses.

Sudinna, a disciple of the Buddha and the only son of a very wealthy family in Vesali, confirmed this teaching. His parents were afraid that if they had no offspring the Licchavis would take over their heirless property. Therefore, the Venerable Sudinna's mother beseeched him to beget a child (and heir) as a seed for future generations. Sudinna acceded to his mother's request and had sexual intercourse with his former wife. (The son thus begotten was called Bijaka, meaning seed.) Afterward, Sudinna suffered remorse because his conscience told him that this violation of celibacy was wrong. He became mentally ill, emaciated and his condition was noticed by his fellow monks. When the true cause of his illness became known, the Buddha laid down, for the first time, the rule that sexual practice is improper for monks.[62]

There is an apparent contradiction between the story of Seyyasaka, which teaches that one who is unhappy with his celibacy may become ill, and the teaching of the Buddha that the failure to practice celibacy will cause illness. Perhaps the resolution of this apparent contradiction lies in this: In one who enters or remains in the celibate life reluctantly and whose sexual desires are not well-controlled, the frustration of the sexual urge may bring or cause illness. But in the person whose spiritual development is such that he willingly chooses to lead a celibate life, the realization that he has failed to attain a pure or perfect celibacy may itself cause illness.

---

[60]The Book of the Discipline (Vinaya-Piṭaka) (Suttavibhanga), Vol. I, translated by I.B. Horner (London: Published for The Pali Text Society by Luzac & Company, LTD., 1949), pp. 193-195.

[61]The Book of the Gradual Sayings (Anguttara-Nikaya), Vol. III, translated by E.M. Hare (London: Published for The Pali Text Society by Luzac & Company, ITD, 1961), p. 110.

[62]See The Book of the Disciple (Vinaya-Piṭaka) (Sutta Vibhanga), Vol. I, translated by I.B. Horner (London: Published for The Pali Text Society, 1949), pp. 21-38.

Only the willing celibate is a proper candidate for ordination, but others may seek it. The monk's unmarried life is individually free. He does not have to undertake any responsibility for marriage or its consequences. A monk can devote all his time and energy to spiritual development. But if he is not active in spiritual practices there is not much special about his monkhood. It is both a waste of time and a painful restraint on his freedom in terms of sexual activity, especially when he longs for it.

A monk who cannot control his sexual urge is allowed to leave the monastic community and live as a householder according to his need. If he remains in the and becomes involved in sexual intercourse, what is the effect on his religious pursuit? According to Buddhist texts, the ordained monk who has violated the moral rule of celibacy loses his monkhood and will fall into a miserable state (hell) after death.

It is also believed that after committing a sexual act, such a monk cannot attain liberation or nirvana. It might be more accurate to say that the violation delays his final goal. He is encouraged to give up his status as a fully-ordained monk (upasampada) and to choose to resume either the role of a novice monk (samanera), or a lay person. If he then devotes himself to the moral precepts and the law (dhamma), it is still possible for him to attain anagamihood (the penultimate stage of enlightenment) or even arahantship (final enlightenment) in this lifetime.

The practice of celibacy is regarded not merely as abstaining from physical sexual acts but as leading to the complete perfection which is the ultimate goal of Buddhist practices: freedom from birth and death and attainment of eternity, nirvana. In other words, for the Buddhist monk, the ultimate aim of the practice of celibacy is to eradicate the mental defilements -- greed, hatred and delusion -- to attain nirvana which is the summum bonum of religious life. The fulfillment of celibacy is the attainment of nirvana.

Given this information, we now understand the origin, structure and development of the Sangha as an independent society. Only laws (dhamma) and disciplinary rules (vinaya) are the governing body of the Sangha. Its religious and institutional activities are shown to be the blueprint or guide to a democratic society.

CHAPTER IV

SECRETARIAT OR SUPREME COURT OF THE SANGHA

Methods of Settling Problems

The Sangha has no particular office or headquarters apart from the vihára or the kuṭi where members dwell. Nor is there any fixed place where opponents can file cases for a legitimate judgment or decision against another party. In ancient times, all controversial cases were handled in the presence of the Buddha in any open place such as a forest or vihára. Most cases were determined by the conference of the laws (dhamma sabhá) in the presence of the Sangha assembly. The focus of attention was directed to the high wisdom and moral conduct of the leaders who determined the cases.

In the vinaya rules, each code was accompanied by a penalty in order to prevent the transgressor from further aberrations from a morally pious path. Similarly, a breach of each rule of right conduct would result in the formulation of a like penalty.[1] Therefore, each rule is the direct outcome of some actual event or incident and not formulated on hypothetical conditions or imaginary situations.

The punishment of an unrepentant monk who deliberately committed an improper act or transgressed the established rules was handed down by the Sangha. Normally, this was done only after he had made a formal and humble request to know the penalty for his offence. This enabled the individual to maintain privacy of moral conscience. In addition, this prevented all possible disputes or conflicts which might otherwise occur and disrupt the tranquillity of the Sangha.

It is believed that whoever commits a transgression and confesses it in accordance with the rules and attains restraint, will achieve growth in the noble norm (dhamma). However, this conscientious moral system does not always work. Sometimes force is required to establish peace.

---

[1]The Book of the Discipline (Vinaya Piṭaka), Vol. I, translated by I.B. Horner (London: Published for the Páli Text Society by Luzac & Company, LTD., 1949), pp. XIV-XV.

There are instances where force was used even during the Buddha's life. On certain occasions he had to order monks to be punished. He even had to banish[2] some from the Sangha permanently. In one classic example, the Buddha ordered the Sangha to impose a higher penalty on a monk named Channa who had acted adversely to the established norm by being obstinate and perverse.[3] The Buddha excommunicated him from the Sangha. This type of punishment served for the obstinate person and even expulsion from the Sangha for a monk who committed a grave or incurable offence (párájiká). However, in modern practice, a more extreme punishment is necessary than the one embodied in the original Vinaya text. For instance, if necessary, the Thai Sangha would accept the aid of the civil authorities in order to expel a monk who violated one of the major rules (párájiká). In order to maintain the health and harmony of the Sangha or any society, compassionate behavior alone is sometimes not enough. Determinative action by the administrators is quite imperative.

Suppose an individual member of the Sangha neglected, or deliberately transgressed the established ethical codes what would happen to him? If he is unfaithful and dishonest, hides the transgression, and has no witnesses against him, then the Sangha can do nothing to him.

There is a couple of ways in which a monk can get away with violating a rule.[4] For instance, if he is the very first monk to transgress that particular rule, he is exempt from punishment. Likewise, if he is mentally or physically ill or if he had no intention of committing the act performed, he is not punished.

A different category of rules was applied for special conditions wherever it was necessary. For example, if a monk was mentally ill, any negative act he performed could be forgiven. There is no vinaya rule which calls for the punishment or persecution of a monk for just thinking in evil or unwholesome

---

[2]Ibid., p. 66; p. 321; p. 328.

[3]Dialogues of the Buddha (Dïgha-Nikáya), Part II, translated by T.W. and C.A.F. Rhys Davids (London: Published for the Páli Text Society by luzac & Company, LTD., 1959), p. 172.

[4]The Book of the Discipline (Vinaya Piṭaka), Vol. II, translated by I.B. Horner, p. 23.

ways. His transgression becomes legitimate only after his evil thought is expressed in words or acts.

Suppose a certain member of the Sangha has transgressed the ethical code but denies it, though there are witnesses. If certain members have seen him violating the code they can directly admonish him to amend it. They can also request that he leave the Sangha, depending on the severity of the violation. If he refuses to do so, then the witnesses must report it to his senior representative, or to the Sangha. Any member of the Sangha is considered to be a representative in such a case. Any member who has seen another monk violating the code can take the step to admonish the monk or report the violation if he wishes to do so. Sometimes even the laity has undertaken the moral task of reporting violation by monks. In some serious cases involving a párájiká or a Sanghádisesa, a monk is expected to volunteer to admonish and report the case. If a monk conceals another monk's serious offence (garukáppatti) he, too, commits an offence.[5]

In reporting a case, usually an authoritative Sangha member summons both parties. The defendant and accuser present themselves for examination amidst the assembly. Upon investigating the case, and verifying the offence, the Sangha metes out the punishment. When proof of the crime is determined, the violator is not punished in the manner one may find in a court of justice. All the Sangha can do to such a dishonest monk is ostracize him. They could also make him an exile.[6] Such a monk will become a notorious person. This is the greatest punishment that the Sangha can formally render according to the Vinaya text.

If a suspended monk went back to his household life, and returned later to request ordination again, the Buddha did not allow his return until the monk accepted the prior offence. "Will you see the offence?" This is the first question to be asked when he requests to be a member of the Sangha again. If he says, "Yes, I will accept it," he can be re-ordained a monk; otherwise, he will not be

---

[5]See Sanghádisesa.

[6]Dialogue of the Buddha (The Dïgha-Nikáya), Part II, translated by T.W. and C.A.F. Rhys Davids, pp. 171-172: One of the exemplary cases of excommunication was that of Channa. The Buddha gave advice to Ánanda about rendering a higher penalty when he said, "'Let Channa say whatever he may like, Ánanda, the brethren should neither speak to him, nor exhort him, nor admonish him."

readmitted.[7] Suppose he does not accept his offence after he has been ordained again, what should his position be? If that is the case, he would not be restored, but would be suspended again. It is necessary to have a unanimous decision within the Sangha for this suspension.

If the offence committed by an individual monk is one of the four defeats (párájikás) he is ostracized immediately. If the offence committed is an amendable one, then upon confessing it he is admonished not to do it again. The penalty is imposed upon him normally with his consent. Upon confessing his offence(s) and after fulfillment of his probation and penalty, he is re-instated to his former position.

Any problem situation can most likely be settled by using one or more of the following three methods: (1) by agreement of the involved parties themselves, (2) by arbitration between individuals/groups and (3) by the power of the Sangha. There is a method of settling problems in the presence (sammukhávinaya) of the assembly of bhikkhus and the accused party. This sammukhávinaya has four sections or factors: (1) the presence of the Sangha (sanghasammukhatá), (2) the presence of laws (dhammasammukhatá), (3) the presence of disciplinary rules and regulations (vinayasammukhatá) and (4) the presence of the person(s) involved (puggalasammukhatá).[8]

When a quarrel or dispute arises between parties it should be handled particularly calmly and wisely. To do this, the Buddha taught seven ways to settle problems and restore harmony and peace. These seven rules are as follows:

(1) Negotiating face to face. This includes a fact finding session or an official hearing in a court. A face to face discussion can clear up the confusion and misunderstanding between the parties.

---

[7]The Book of the Discipline (Mahávagga), translated by I.B. Horner, pp. 125-126.

[8]Somdet Phra Maha Samana Chao Krom Phraya Vajirañánavaroras, compiled, The Entrance to the Vinaya Vinayamukha, Vol. I (Bangkok: Mahámakut Rájavidyálaya Press, 2526/1983), p. 141.

(2) Appealing to the conscience. This is a process of detached and objective consideration, or a genuine consultation of one's own consciousness. Sometimes such a process makes one realize the facts, thus creating the solution to the problem. Though it may require sacrifices from an individual it is not impossible to follow the conscience.

(3) Negotiating with a clear mind. Confusions disappear when a clear recognition of the facts has taken place. As a result, any problem which occurred due to cloudy thinking is solved.

(4) Confession. Confession is the obvious step towards solving the problem. There is nothing secret about it. When one confesses one's fault the other party will determine whether to take action or to forgive.

(5) Majority vote of the chapter. In a contest of different parties, the majority vote is often honored. It brings about a solution to the problem. (It is clear that the word, "chapter," referred to a group of authoritative people from all parties involved.)

(6) There must be the existence of a specific offence or violation of an enacted law or norm as well as an actual proof that an offence or fault was committed.

(7) Hiding a fault.[9] This is an attempt to overlook an offence which has been committed. This is not the best way to solve the problem, but sometimes it does solve it. At least it prevents it from aggravating and creating greater problems. According to the situation, time and place, by using one or more of these rules, disputes can be settled.

[9]The Book of the Gradual Sayings (The Anguttara-Nikáya), Vol. IV, translated by E.M. Hare (London: Published for the Páli Text Society by Luzac & Company, LTD., p. 97.

A monk wishing to be a qualified judge[10] must possess various qualities. He must be virtuous and possess restraint. In addition, he must be proficient in following the practice of good conduct, should know right from wrong, possess impartial judgment, be learned, competent, and capable to correctly comprehend legal matters. He must be able to analyze cases in detail, make both parties in a dispute recognize the facts and help to reconcile the situation. Finally, he should be skilled in the causes and settlements of disputes and especially know the matter at issue, the cause of its occurrence, and the way to end it.[11] These confession and correction procedures are very important factors embodied in the Vinaya texts.

Confession and Amendment

The Buddhist monks have been strongly advised by the Buddha to gather at least once a year as a congregational whole. At this time, each member of the Sangha should make a formal declaration amidst the assembly: "if anybody has seen, heard or suspected any action done by me against standard moral conduct, please tell me so that I will amend it at once and recognize it." This open minded invitation provides fellow monks with the best opportunity to reprove each other if they deserve it. Also, it is a good opportunity for each person to learn about and understand himself better. He gets to find out what others think of his moral character and behavior.

We cannot learn about ourselves unless we are open; thus, there is a need to share others' ideas. When we openly risk evaluation by our colleagues and companions, the rewards are discovery, growth and achievement. This is just like an evaluation of a school teacher. Sometimes we intentionally act in a way our companions dislike. Therefore, moral evaluation or invitation (paváraná) is essential to developing friendly terms and harmony. If we could utilize the same process for our present world, we might remove hostility and harmoniously strengthen social unity.

---

[10]The Book of the Gradual Sayings (Anguttara-Nikáya), Vol. V, translated by F.L. Woodward (London: Published for the Páli Text Society by Luzac & Company, LTD., 1961), p. 51.

[11]Ibid., p. 52.

Showing the advantages of such an invitation, the Buddha himself said that "sá vo bhavissati aññamaññánulomatá ápattivutthánatá vinayapurekkháratá."[12] The Buddhist monks have been instructed to perform this paváraná in a specific manner. A monk should neatly place his upper robe on his left shoulder, sit on his haunches properly, and join both palms together in a respectful manner. Then, he may make any humble request. The passage explains that he should invite the Sangha three times by saying:

> samghaṁ ávuso paváremi ditthena vá sutena vá parisankáya vá, vadantu man áyasmanto anukampaṁ upádáya, passanto patikarissámi.[13]

This procedure is followed in the hope of removing offenses (ápattivutthánatá), and to better understand or fulfill the disciplinary rules and regulations (vinayapurekkháratá).[14] If there is a complete quorum of members in residence, each monk according to seniority should repeat this request in the midst of the complete assembly. If necessary, he may perform this ritual with only one other monk. If he is the only monk present in his residence, then he should make a resolution that that day is the invitation (paváraná) day. With regard to such an invitation, the whole Pávaraná Section in The Mahávagga may be made as a reference here.

The traditional Buddhist custom of asking for forgiveness is still being carried out in Buddhist countries. Traditionally, this act takes place once a year at the end of the rain retreat on full moon day, in October. However, forgiveness

---

[12]"It would be suitable for you in respect to living a communal life to remove offenses and to acquire discipline as part of the fundamental practice." Hermann Oldenberg, ed., The Vinaya Piṭakaṁ (The Mahávagga), Vol. I (London: Published for the Páli Text Society by Luzac & Company, LTD., 1964), p. 159.

[13]"Your revered sirs, I invite the Sangha in regard to what has been seen (ditthena) or heard (sutena) or doubted (parisankáya). Your honored sirs, tell me out of compassion, and any error upon seeing it I will make amends." The Vinaya Pitakam (the Mahávagga), Vol. I, p. 159.

[14]The Book of the Discipline (Mahávagga), translated by I.B. Horner, p. 211ff.

can be asked for and granted at anytime. Whenever the wrong-doer realizes that he has done wrong he may be forgiven.

If the offence is serious, then the offender must observe the prescribed steps of the <u>paváraná</u>. Once these humble steps have been performed, he then addresses his teacher or preceptor in the following manner: "Your Venerable Sir, with my arrogance I have done such and such things against you by my three doors (<u>dvárattayena</u>): mouth, body and mind. Please kindly forgive me for all." The senior monk replies, "Never mind, you should guard yourself properly," or, "I forgive you. If there is any offence done by me against you, please forgive me also." In this way their companionship becomes harmonious and beautiful.

If the wrong-doer is senior to the other monk he simply asks the junior's forgiveness. He can forego without saluting, kneeling down, or joining palms. The reply will be the same. In any case, the request for forgiveness should be made in a sincerely conciliatory manner. This is considered to be a very beautiful custom of confession and amendment in Buddhism.

This custom is not revered only by Buddhists. This is basic human ethics. It is applicable to anyone who is ardently good and humane, civilized and cultured, and desiring the harmonious union of mankind. The Buddha rebuked those who praised themselves and criticized others. He did not support those who angered people and were unforgiving to those who had transgressed. Of course, the manner of asking and giving forgiveness may be varied according to the culture or society. The aims and essence remain the same.

Everyone has had the experience of saying, "I am sorry," "Excuse me," "I beg your pardon," or "I apologize...," We do this from time to time when a wrong has intentionally or unintentionally been committed. Sometimes this method of confession establishes a mutual understanding. It helps to strengthen the harmonious union with associates or friends. It creates a chance to improve or develop human ethology. The custom of asking for forgiveness and granting it ought to be carried out continuously according to the milieu and self realization of error. It does not matter whether those offenses are light or grave ones. Upon being humbly petitioned, forgiveness should be granted to the offender.

Asking and granting forgiveness are always essential for both parties. These acts erase conflicts and contentions, as well as console, restrengthen and restore harmony and peace. Sometimes, when a genuine confession is put forth, the confessor of even a slight error is looked down upon cynically and contemptuously. The Buddha prohibited such behavior.

An offender is not always bad. Sometimes he has committed offenses out of ignorance; he will become a better man when he realizes that he has done wrong. The Buddha instructed his monks not to curse or tease a person about an offence that had been committed. This was instituted so that the offender would no longer be held under the condition and would be free from it. It was not to be mentioned even as a joke. If someone made fun by referring to someone else's error, he in turn would commit an offence of wrong-doing (dukkaṭa). The Buddha said that upon request for forgiveness (for slight offenses) the offender should immediately be forgiven. Those who would not see their fault, and those who would not forgive were regarded as fools. He called those wise who acted otherwise.[15]

This is the constitution of confession and amendment which is imperative to the Sangha as well as to any humanistic community, or ideal society.

Schism and Resolution Within the Sangha

The cause of a conflict can be as a match burning an entire forest. Similarly, man's greed and anger can consume the entire world! Let us consider how a conflict within the religious community can begin with a trifling matter and develop into an immense ordeal.

Once a quarrel arose among monks in Kosambi regarding the violation of a disciplinary rule. Eventually, this quarrel split the Order of monks and the lay disciples into two factions. The Buddha tried to end the quarrel and reconcile the

---

[15]The Book of the Gradual Sayings (Anguttara-Nikáya), Vol. I, translated by F.L. Woodward (London: Published for the Páli Text Society by Luzac & Company, LTD., 1970), p. 54.

groups but he was unsuccessful. Finally, he left the Sangha. He went alone to a forest to meditate. The detailed story of the conflict is as follows:

At one time the Buddha was residing at Kosambi in Ghosita's monastery.[16] At the same place there were two monks who each had a following of five hundred. At the monastery one of these monks fell into an offence. Although he did not realize his fault, other monks recognized it as an offence. After a while, the one who had committed the offence accepted their judgment. Later the monks changed their opinion on the matter.[17] The group of monks obtaining unanimity excommunicated him for not admitting his fault. At this point the conflict began. The paraphrased passage of the Dhammapada Commentary gives a clearer view of this matter as follows:

One of two opposing monks was an expert at discipline (vinayadhara). The other was a preacher of the good law (dhammakathika). The preacher, after using the latrine one day, left some water[18] in a container. He had used the container to wash in the bathroom. The vinayadhara monk went into the latrine and saw the left over water. When he came out he inquired of his companion, by saying, "Brother (avuso), was it you who left the water in the vessel in the latrine?" "Yes, brother," he replied. "But do you not know that it is an offence (apattibhavan) to do so?" "No, I do not." "Brother, it is an offence (apatti)," replied the Vinayadhara. "Then I will amend (patikarissami) it," said the dhammakathika. "Brother, if you did it without intention (asancicca), without mindfulness (asatiya)

---

[16]The Book of the Discipline (Mahavagga), Vol. IV, translated by I.B. Horner (London: Luzac & Company, LTD., 1962), p. 483: This text does not mention the two quarrelling monks' specific title as vinayadhara and Dhammakathika, definite nature of offence committed and the number of their retinues. The Dhammapada Commentary makes all these points clear but it does not mention that whether the Buddha was in Ghosita's monastery together with those quarrelling monks.

[17]The Book of the Discipline (Mahavagga), I.B. Horner, p. 483.

[18]According to the disciplinary rule, if a monk knowingly and intentionally leaves water in the container in the latrine it is considered to be an offence of wrong-doing (dukkata). But if a monk does it without knowing, without intention, then it is considered to be no offence.

it is not an offence," clarified the Vinayadhara. Thus the preacher of the law came to accept it as no offence. He did it without intent.

Later though, the monk who was an expert at discipline told his pupils, "This preacher of the good law does not know an offence when he has committed it." Approaching one of the pupils of the Vinayadhara the monk teased by saying, "Your preceptor does not even know when he has committed an offence." The pupils of the preacher went back and informed him. The preacher told his pupils, "Before this Vinayadhara monk said, "It is no offence." Now he says, "It is an offence. He is a liar." Thus, an unnecessary misunderstanding took place between them. The different factions approached each other and taunted one another. The pupils of the preacher said, "Your teacher is a liar." A quarrel began between the two teachers.[19] The preacher of the good law was excommunicated.

The excommunicated monk was very erudite. He was a receiver of the tradition handed down, an expert in dhamma, discipline (vinaya), and the summaries (ágatágama).[20] The preacher approached his comrades, and saying, "What I have done is not an offence. I have not fallen into an offence. Their excommunication of me is not legally valid. It is not fit to stand. It is reversible. Therefore, venerable sirs, please be on my side because of the rule and discipline." He gathered many friends as his partisans. At the same time, he sent messengers to other monks who were staying in the countryside and elsewhere. He was successful in gathering more and more support until many monks rallied for him[21]. They approached the other party and chastised them by saying, "Your reverend sirs, this is not an offence. He has not fallen into nor committed any offence. This innocent monk was suspended by you for a formal act that is reversible."[22] The other party strongly rebutted them by saying, "Your reverend sirs, this is an

---

[19]Buddhist Legends (Dhammapada Commentary), Part I, translated by Eugene Watson Burlingame (London: Published for the Páli Text Society by Luzac & Company, LTD., 1969), p. 176.

[20]The Book of the Discipline (Mahávagga), translated by I.B. Horner (London: Luzac & Company, LTD., 1951), p. 483.

[21]Ibid.

[22]Ibid., p. 484.

offence... Therefore, he is excommunicated by a formal act that was legally valid; do not side with him." The supporters of the dhammakathika monk did not listen and sided with him anyhow.

The story adds the hyperbolic information that even the protector Gods (devas), and the deities dwelling in the sky, the world of Brahma, in fact all beings, even the unconverted ones sided with one of the two factions. The dispute extended to the realm of the four great kings and even up to the heaven of the Gods Sublime![23]

Finally, a monk approached the Buddha and reported the whole story. Upon hearing this matter, he immediately sent a message for them to reconcile and unite. Evidently, they failed to obey. The Buddha realized that the Sangha might split asunder.[24] He approached the monks who had excommunicated the monk asking them to reverse their decision. He explained that in such an intense situation their action would only cause dissention within the Sangha. Moreover, he said that a monk who sees that a schism is likely should not excommunicate another monk for failing to recognize an offence.[25] He pointed out the mistake involved in their action.

The Buddha then went to visit the allies of the excommunicated monk. He asked them to amend the offence which had been committed, and thereby solve the problem. He explained that failing to do so would create a schism. He explained the danger in pushing the Sangha towards a schism. Finally, he asked that the offence be confessed out of faith to the other monks.[26]

The Buddha advised both monks to hold an uposatha and other formal acts within the boundary (sīma). He established the disciplinary rule that monks who

---

[23]Buddhist Legends (The Dhammapada Commentary), Part I, translated by Eugene Watson Burlingame, p. 176.

[24]Ibid., pp. 176-177.

[25]The Book of the Discipline (Mahávagga), translated by I.B. Horner, p. 485.

[26]Ibid., p. 486.

quarreled in the refectory or anywhere ought to stay in separate seats.[27] At that time, the monks who favored the excommunicated monk held the uposatha right within the boundary. The other group held the uposatha and other formal acts outside the boundary. This created an even deeper rift within the Sangha.

Despite the Buddha's instruction the monks could not stop fighting. They lambasted one another with verbal assaults (mukhasatthīhi). They behaved improperly in a refectory amidst the lay people, assaulted one another with provocative gestures, and even came to blows.

Lay people criticized the monks and looked down upon them. The Buddha instructed them never to do that kind of stupid behavior again. He said,

> Promise in your heart, thinking, "At least we will not
> behave improperly to one another in gesture and
> speech; more importantly we will never come to
> blows."[28]

The Buddha struggled to end the conflict. He told them of the disadvantages and dangers of quarrels. He recounted the story of Játaka and the tiny quail (The Játaka, Vol. III, pp. 174-177). He used this story to illustrate the danger involved in quarrelling. In the story, a tiny quail brought about the destruction of a noble elephant on account of a quarrel. He warned them that thousands of quails lost their lives in the battle (The Játaka, Vol. I, pp. 208-210).

The monks failed to heed his advice. In fact, a heretical monk (adhammavádin) advised the Buddha, "Venerable sir, let you the Lord, the dhamma master, remain at home unconcerned. Live a life of ease in this world now. We will be responsible for ourselves. We will make ourselves notorious with our strife."[29]

---

[27]Buddhist Legends, Part I, p. 177.

[28]The Book of the Discipline (Mahávagga), p. 488.

[29]Ibid., p. 489; see also The Buddhist Legends, Part I, p. 177.

According to legend, the Buddha made countless attempts to reach a settlement. He used many stories and parables as examples of the danger quarrels could create. As an example he told them the story of Brahmadatta, the powerful and wealthy king of Kasi. Dïghiti, King of Kosala, was poor and powerless and Brahmadatta captured his kingdom and killed him. Prince Dïghávu, son of Dïghiti, became a trusted friend of Brahmadatta. He spared Brahmadatta's life when he had a good chance to kill him.[30] Because of this attitude, King Brahmadatta and Prince Dïghávu made peace with each other. The Buddha clearly pointed out the patience and gentleness of Dïghávu.

The Buddha encouraged the ordained monks to "set their light to shine in this world as the result of practicing patience and gentleness." He expressed his negative opinions on conflict and war and admonished the monks, all without success.[31]. The Dhammapada Commentary adds information that the Buddha was jostled under the crowded conditions and finally departed.

The Buddha dressed himself in a saffron robe. He collected his bowl and upper robe (sanghāti). He walked round for alms collection in Kosambi. In the midst of the Sangha, he expressed the notion that it was better to dwell alone in a solitary place rather than living with foolish men. He left the assembly to live alone in the village of Balakalonakara.

On his way to Parileyyaka via the Eastern Bamboo Grove he taught the bliss of union to some youths and later taught amity to monks. He gradually approached Parileyyaka where he stayed in the Protected Woodland Thicket (Rakkhitavanasanda). At the foot of the beautiful Sal-tree, he spent the rainy season (vassávása). He lived with an elephant[32] and a monkey.[33] The Buddha felt relieved and more relaxed. He was able to meditate there.

---

[30]The Book of the Discipline (Mahávagga), p. 496.

[31]Ibid., p. 498.

[32]Buddhist Legends, p. 178.

[33]Ibid., p. 180.

The quarrel continued for some time. The Buddha's absence became more evident to the monks and lay people. Lay devotees of Kosambi went to the monastery and did not see the Buddha. When they found out the entire story from the monks and understood that the Buddha's efforts to reunite them were in vain, the people became very upset, even disenchanted. Resenting the troublesome monks, they realized the folly of what had happened. The people felt that, "because of these monks we cannot see the Buddha." Further, they replied that, since "these monks did not want to patch up their differences, we will not pay them respect. We will not give them any financial support, or gifts (dána)."[34] People did not show the monks any signs of much civility. When they stopped offering their generosity and respect, the monks of Kosambi realized the gravity of the situation.

These reactions brought a very challenging situation to the Sangha. The monks, having hardly any food, were almost famished[35] within a few days and began to feel humiliated. At this point, a reconciliation between the Sangha became necessary. So the quarrel was put aside. The monks started to call one another to confess their offenses. However, they had to spend the rainy season uncomfortably until the Buddha rectified it.[36]

Some monks went to see the Buddha for advice, wanting to reconcile for good in his presence. The lay followers forced them to do so since the loss of their support system had a devastating effect, which in turn resulted in their effort to find peace.

---

[34]Buddhist Legends, Part I, p. 178; see also The Book of the Discipline (Mahávagga), p. 505.

[35]It is clear that because those monks quarrelled lay followers lost their faith in them. However, they might have continuously supported the monks but only to one's own party. Because of this and sectarian activity their financial situation was apparently desperate and it became hard for them to maintain themselves.

[36]Normally, a monk is supposed to stay in a dwelling, without spending the night(s) at another place, during the three months of the rainy reason (beginning around July and ending in October of a year). Violation of this rule is an offence of wrong-doing (dukkata).

A group of five hundred non-political monks went to see the Buddha in the forest. They desired to hear <u>dhamma</u> from him. So he allowed them to come.[37] These monks expressed their concern that "The Buddha was very delicate. He must have faced hardship and difficulty while staying alone in the forest. He has had no attendants to do his major and minor duties." The Buddha assured them that the Parileyyaka elephant attended him. He had a pleasant time and in that context, he taught them that it was better to live alone with the elephant than to live with a simpleton. As a result of this teaching, five hundred monks realized truth and attained arahatship.[38]

Many lay disciples of Kosambi, as well as eminent lay disciples of Savatthi, such as Anáthapindika and Visákhá, were eager to see the Buddha as soon as possible. The venerable Änanda conveyed the message to the Buddha saying, "Your venerable sir, fifty million noble disciples including their chief, Anáthapindika, want you to come back to Savatthi."[39] He accepted the invitation to Savatthi and stayed in Jetavana.

The two groups of monks went to Savatthi to see him and to ask for forgiveness. It was very hard for them to obtain a visa for their journey (i.e., the King of Kosala did not want the quarrelsome monks to enter his country). However, the Buddha persuaded the king that the monks were good men. He explained that they were coming to request his forgiveness. He asked the king to allow them to come.[40] The king permitted them to enter. Likewise, although Anáthapindika did not want the monks in his monastery, he could not prohibit them from living there.

When the monks arrived in Savatthi the Buddha requested that the head monk arrange for separate lodgings. They were not allowed to associate with the other company until they were officially and completely reconciled. It is interesting

---

[37]<u>Buddhist Legends</u>, pp. 180-181.

[38]<u>Buddhist Legends</u>, pp. 181-182.

[39]Ibid., p. 182.

[40]Ibid., p. 183.

to note that upon hearing this news many people were excited. The news inspired many people to visit the Buddha to see the monks seeking his forgiveness.

The Buddha acknowledged their sins (pápa). Many monks, nuns and lay devotees went to visit him, seeking his advice on how to behave with regard to the monks. He advised that they listen carefully both parties and decide which spoke the truth (dhamma) correctly and then they were to act accordingly (yathádhammo tathá tiṭṭháhi).[41] He advised them to remain unprejudiced to either party and asked them to give gifts (dána) to both parties.

It is interesting to note that after all the trouble, the excommunicated monk came to, he realized his fault. He realized that his suspension was legally valid! Therefore, he approached the monks who suspended him and confessed his offence. He apologized and humbly requested them to restore him to monkhood. These monks requested the Buddha's advice in regards to this case.

The monk was restored; thus, the unanimity of the Sangha was restored by means of a formal motion. In the midst of the assembly, the Pátimokkha was recited at once; providing a symbol of the formal and legal unification of the Sangha in accordance with the vinaya rules.

In response to Upáli's, (an expert on vinaya rules) question, the Buddha said that an investigation should be made concerning the actual reason for the restoration of unanimity. Lip service alone would not be sufficient. The reason for the return to harmony, and the formality of its re-emergence must be stated clearly in order for the unanimity to be legally valid. Thus, the schism was resolved and concord was re-established.[42] Happy is the harmony and union of the Sangha.

The Requirements and Allowance of Possessions

No monk can possess any private property whatsoever. Only absolute necessities are allowed, such as a begging bowl and a set of saffron robes which

---

[41]The Book of the Discipline (Mahávagga), pp. 505-507.

[42]Ibid., pp. 509-512.

he wears. If he keeps anything extra,[43] for longer than ten days, he commits an offence of expiation. He must forfeit the extra items to the Sangha on the eleventh day at sunrise.[44] He must also undergo punishment under the confession of expiation (pácittiya) rule. The Sangha is the automatic heir of any extra possessions and allots them to individual members on the basis of need.[45]

If one or more of a monk's three robes is destroyed (or lost) a monk can accept another. If he asks for more it is a wrong-doing (dukkata). Therefore, when an extra robe is acquired, it must be forfeited to the Sangha, to a group, or to another monk.

To forfeit it he should follow a systematic routine. A monk should formally say:

> idaṁ me bhante cïvaraṁ aññátakaṁ gahapatikaṁ
> upasamkamitvá tat'uttariṁ viññápitaṁ nissaggiyaṁ,
> imáhaṁ saṁghassa nissajjámïti...[46]

---

[43]The Buddha allowed or rather required a monk to possess as his personal property eight requisites. They are: (1) a bowl (patta) in which to collect almsfood for his maintenance, (2) a double layer cloak (sangháti) which a monk usually puts on his left shoulder, (3) a single layer robe (uttarásanga), also called cïvara) to cover his body, (4) an under robe or garment (antaravásaka), (5) a belt (káyabandhana) to tie his waist, (6) a needle to sew his robes, (7) a thread, (8) and a water-filter so that he may not drink water with living animals.

[44]The Book of the Discipline (Mahávagga), pp. 4-5: Without being asked (if somebody voluntarily offers) a monk can accept any amount of robes, or any other proper things. But his motivation should not be in accumulating material things for himself but to give them to the Sangha or fellow monks who need them. With the intention to help others, venerable Änanda accepted five hundred robes at one time. Yet there was no offence ascribed to him.

[45]The Book of the Discipline (Vinaya Pitaka), Vol. II, translated by I.B. Horner, p. XXXII.

[46]"Venerable sirs, having gone up to a lay person who is not my relation, this robe asked for by me more than I am permitted to have is to be forfeited.

This is a challenge for a materially inclined monk who shamelessly asks for a robe from a householder who is not his relative.

No monk should have any storehouse or lodging[47] which is not open to other members of the Sangha. If a monk builds his hut without bringing the required quorum of monks to mark the site, an offence is committed. The Sangha will attach a serious penalty to the offence.

The Buddha did not allow monks to physically handle any sort of currency, including gold and silver.[48]

Therefore, I forfeit it to the Sangha." Hermann Oldenberg, ed., The Vinaya Piṭakaṁ (The Suttavibhanga), Vol. III (London: Published for the Páli Text Society by Luzac & Company, LTD., 1964), pp. 214-215: Here the Buddha is to have said that the Sangha or individual monk who receives the forfeited robe should give it back to the monk who has forfeited it to him.   But here the compassionate recommendation that the forfeited article be given back to one who has committed the offence amounts to allowing that this rule can be abolished. Because when a monk has possessed or accumulated more robes than he is permitted to, he is considered to have violated the rule and then he should forfeit it to the Sangha or another monk. But when that article is given back to him he again has the same exceeding number of robes. Therefore, it stands to reason that the monk who has committed the offence and who has forfeited the robe to the Sangha or to another monk should not receive the article even if he is kindly given it back should he wish to maintain this rule.

[47]If some laity voluntarily offers a monk, without his asking, he can accept monasteries or mansions. Otherwise, he is not permitted to make by himself even a hut larger than twelve spans in length and seven spans in width (The Book of the Discipline (Vinaya Piṭaka), Vol. I, translated by I. B. Horner, p. 353).   The Buddha held such individual offering as less important when he said such a donor gets less merit than he is deserved to get if he were to offer the same object to the Sangha community.   The Middle Length Sayings (Majjhima-Nikáya), Vol. III, translated by I.B. Horner (London: Published for the Páli Text Society by Luzac & Company, LTD., 1967), p. 300ff.

[48]The Book of the Discipline (Vinaya Pitaka), Vol. II, p. 102.

87

A monk can eat his meal[49] only before noon or at midday. He must remain celibate at all times. If he eats food in the afternoon he will be punished. The Sangha members are not allowed to privatize and use as personal property the community's belongings such as pots, pans and, like things made of iron. If a monk does so, a dukkaṭa offence will fall upon him. Hence, monks must use all community property in common. Does this philosophy sound like that of a communist? Or does it sound like Plato's requirements for the ruling class of his ideal republic government? This is an explanation of monastic community life. Detachment is the social power in monastic life.

In the context of the monk's social power, which he possesses through his being detached to worldly objects, the Buddha puts his monk in the list of noble prince at the present of King Pasenadi of Kosala. Here the monk is one of the creatures in the world that must not be lightly regarded in their youth. King Pasenadi rejoiced upon and was very impressed by this advice of the Buddha. He was later converted to Buddhism.[50]

For the purpose of practicing detachment, the robe-fund or money given by a lay person to buy robes was not accepted directly by a monk.[51] A request of

---

[49]There are no dietary restrictions for a monk except intoxicants. The Buddha allowed monks to eat fish and meat which were pure in three conscientious respects: while being killed, the animals were not seen, nor heard by that monk, nor did he have any doubt that it was killed on the purpose of feeding him. The Book of the Discipline (Mahávagga), translated by I.B. Horner, P. 325. It is obvious then that a monk cannot give the order to intentionally kill an animal for him. For this reason the Buddha forbade Moggallana to invert the earth to let his fellow monks who suffered a famine in Veranja, to enjoy the nutritive essence of the water plants beneath the earth. The Buddha prohibited him from doing so, because by this act "living beings may meet with derangement" (The Book of the Discipline (Vinaya-Piṭaka), Vol. I, translated by I.B. Horner, p. 14)." It seemed that the Buddha did not mind even when he had to eat but horse food, pattha measure of steamed grain (Ibid., p. 12.).

[50]The Book of the Kindred Sayings (Samyutta-Nikáya), Part I, pp. 93-96.

[51]The Book of the Discipline (Vinaya-Piṭaka), Vol. II, p. 65.

King Seniya Bimbisara of Magadha[52] by the Buddha allowed monks to appoint an attendant who would attend to him or his monastery.[53]

If an attendant failed to return the robe-fund that was entrusted to him for a monk, the monk had to make a gesture in order for it to be returned. If the attendant does not give it to him, then he may make a silent protest by standing in front of the guilty person's quarters up to a limit of six times. If the monk is still unsuccessful in obtaining it, then he can go and report it to the donor of the robe-fund.[54] However, the Buddha advised monks to abstain from earning things in a crooked manner. A monk who has renounced his household life for the sake of nibbána should not attach himself to any terrestrial things. Hence, there is one way to gain material things while there is another way to gain nibbána.[55] A monk with noble morals experiences the bliss of blamelessness. He is free like a bird wherever he goes.[56] A content monk is happy even without possessions.

For the Sangha members an office is where they perform their duties. A court is where cases are decided. In a period of science and high technology, with the help of computers, people can run their office without a pen and paper. Similarly, the Sangha used to carry on its affairs and activities even without a proper secretariat headquarters, or court house. The efficacy of the Sangha government is more the result of good laws (dhamma), disciplinary rules (vinaya), moral administration, wisdom and the expertise of its members than of having lots of material resources or high technological equipment.

We have seen how the Buddhist system deals with affairs and problems within the Sangha. Confession and correction are described as necessary factors

---

[52]The Book of the Discipline (Mahávagga), pp. 281-282.

[53]Ibid., p. 127.

[54]Ibid., p. 66.

[55]The Dhammapada, 5:16.

[56]The Book of the Gradual Sayings (Anguttara-Nikáya), Vol. V, translated by F.L. Woodward (London: Published for the Páli Text Society by Luzac & Company, LTD., 1961), 143-144.

for the improvement of personal character and social harmony. The problem of a schism is resolved by confession of the offence (ápatti), and by acting with mutual understanding. A democratic nature is one of the key elements in distributing material gains in the Sangha as well. This is how a democratic government with ethical values should function. Through the autonomy of an ethical system that promotes harmony and peace, an ideal society is possible.

CHAPTER V

CONCLUSION: THE DEMOCRATIC NATURE OF THE SANGHA

The Buddha was from a royal family of the warrior caste. Since he was heir
to the throne in the Sakya kingdom, he was naturally brought into close
association with kings, princes and ministers. Even so, he never tried to seize any
political power, nor did he try to promulgate his teachings through political
campaigning. The Buddha, with profound compassion, and with spiritual guidance
and care helped the Sangha. He never thought of getting back anything like honor
or prestige nor did he have any attachment even to his leadership.

If anybody thinks that the Buddha would carry on the Sangha or that it was
under his direction, it is a wrong estimation. The Buddha said "it never occurred
to him that he would carry on the Sangha or that it was under his direction."[1]
This is an example of the truly detached nature of the leader. His leadership made
it possible for the ideal society to prevail. If we can use this pattern and provide
such genuine service to society, we may also be able to create an ideal society.

The Buddha's policy was to make a detached and sober judgment concerning
the rights of the leader and the individual members. In strictly defined modern
language, hesitation would be counseled in ascribing to the Buddha the role or title
of an absolute egalitarian politician. The Buddha paid attention to the feelings of
the elders, respected their right to authority and was concerned about their
progress as much as that of the younger ones.

The Buddha tried to eliminate or abolish the social classes which he thought
were unfair and unnecessary for the well being of society. The application of
ethics was essential to his political system. He taught that enduring patience is the
highest austerity,[2] non-violence the best act (ahimsá paramo dhammo).
Nonetheless, it requires a great sacrifice to accomplish something using this system.

---

[1]The Book of the Kindred Sayings (Sanyutta-Nikáya), Part V, translated by F.
L. Woodward (London: Published for the Páli Text Society by Luzac & Company,
LTD., 1956), p. 132.

[2]The Dhammapada, 14:6.

91

Ethical conduct (sīla) can be viewed as one of the implementations for voluntarily controlling oneself from unethical actions. It aids people in moving toward mental peace, spiritual development and an increased social harmony. The Buddhist ethical approach to human problems is inductive rather than deductive, particular rather than general. Thus, Buddhist ethical conduct concerns itself with individual and societal problems and their solutions.

The moral philosophy tells us that secular progress and mental peace are interrelated. Without them, life is miserable. All Buddhist scholars easily recognize the importance of this philosophy.   Secular development and spiritual progress should go hand in hand. This is the only way modernization can be successful and the social order established on an ethical philosophy without being undermined. "Pāṇātipāto adinnādānaṁ musā-vādo ca vuccati, para-dāragamanañceva nappasaṁsanti panditā iti."[3] Greed, hatred, and delusion are the main roots of all sorts of immorality.   Killing causes the killer to develop a harsher mentality towards life. All negative aspects of ethical conduct are committed with the mind predominant in one of these three roots; lust or greed (lobha), hatred (dosa) and delusion (moha).   All positive aspects of ethical conduct are performed with the mind dominated by one of three wholesome roots, generosity (alobha), amity (adosa), and wisdom (amoha).

In order to maintain an individual's peace and happiness, the Buddha laid down ethical codes for the Sangha.   Should the Sangha, or society, follow this ethical conduct there would be less conflict, less mental agitation, and more mutual confidence and good will within society.

The system of Buddhist moral principles is very altruistic and democratic in nature.   To be able to strengthen and utilize the ethical values effectively, one is required to be dutiful. Ethical philosophy not only ensures fruitful and pleasant social interaction, but also results in some harmonious integration by society. By strengthening people's faith in and making them understand the value of life,

---

[3]"Killing, stealing, committing sexual misbehavior, and false speech are considered to be disgraceful. A wise person never praises such actions." Estlin Carpenter, ed., The Dïgha-Nikáya, Vol. III (London: Published for the Páli Text Society by Henry Frowde, Oxford University Press Warehouse, 1911), p. 182.

ethical philosophy aims to help prevent people from committing crimes or demerits (pápa or akusala).

Buddhist philosophy maintains that peace and harmony remain among human beings who work actively to achieve such a goal. It is very important to use one's inherent creativity to serve the whole of society by spreading harmony and justice. The state of mutual love, the recognition of the truth, our trust and inter-dependence all contribute integrally to peace. Suspicion, mistrust, disrespect, and injustice lead to conflict and war. Peace is a process of trust and mutual effort to solve problems. This includes bringing the parts of a whole into a strenuously harmonious union of individuals, societies, nations, and the planetary community. One can assume that it is the nature of human beings to occasionally resort to conflict or violence to settle a problem, but real peace cannot be achieved on earth through violence or threats.

It is through sacrifice that people strengthen their friendships and gain peace. For this to be possible sincerity, generosity, and understanding are required. The continuation of relationships and of life on earth is based upon the ability to achieve mutual understanding, acceptance, and a collaboration in the peace process. The Buddha encouraged his followers to recognize human potential in making peace. The cumulative effect of individuals', nations', and the world's expansion of the peace process (mettá) will be the gradual salvaging of human resources from destructive purposes. When it is recognized that all human beings are part of one brotherhood on earth, then their resources to build global peace can be mobilized.

Buddhist ethics are connected to a social political philosophy. In the ethical sense, when a Buddhist talks about progress in life, he is talking about the development not only of an increase in material possessions but also of spiritual possessions. Without concord (sámaggi), neither the Sangha, nor society, is stable. Without change, there is no development in the society. Development and concord must go hand in hand in order to have peace in the society. For Buddhists, ethics constitutes not merely a purely theoretical study of moral phenomena but includes the daily political and non-political realms. One can understand that peace is something more than just the absence of conflict. Peace is an infrastructure of positive harmless acts. Political peace must be the result of efficient acts and the skillful administration of power over many concerns.

Ethics, if accepted as principle, may successfully help to assimilate the diversities into an ideal world. Thus prosperous development as such is important for each individual, and the whole human race longs for it. Without moral ethics, human beings exist without a peaceful state of mind (which can even lead to a state of mutual destruction). In order to sustain peace and happiness, ethical conduct can be integrated into the socio-political structure that affects the conduct and ethical values of society. Buddhist philosophy offers satisfactory explanations of human life and the world. Ethical practice is one of the fundamental factors that enables people to establish an ideal society.

The Buddha did not condemn men to be inferior to him. Rather he showed man a way to the ultimate goal, nibbána and moreover, explained how he himself reached that point. Thus from the very beginning Buddhism's emphasis was on equality and improvement of all.

The Buddha's system of ordaining men as bhikkhus respected freedom of speech and allowed within the Sangha an acceptance of a majority vote. People from all classes or castes can live and operate well with one another in the Sangha because of the disciplinary codes used to regulate the outward conduct of the individual member and the collective practice of the Sangha. These rules or codes apply equally to all the members even the leader of the Sangha. The Buddha practiced what he preached. He said, "yathávádï bhikkhave tathágato tathákárï yathákárï tathágato tathávádï".[4] This emphasizes the democratic nature in the disciplinary rules. He did not just make laws for others and make exception for himself.

There is no room for bias in arbitrating cases. Hence the qualified arbitrator must be free from all bias (agati) as mentioned in the methods of settling problems. Here one can see the elements of democratic nature which may be

---

[4]"Monks! As the tathágata declared so he did. As the tathágata did so he declared." Ernst Windisch, ed., Iti-Vuttaka (Published for the Páli Text Society by Geoffrey Cumberlege, Oxford University Press, 1948), p. 122; T.W. Rhys Davids and J. Estlin Carpenter, eds., The Dïgha-Nikáya, Vol. II (London: Geoffrey Cumberlege, Oxford University Press, 1947), p. 224; see also Dines Andersen and Helmer Smith, eds., Sutta-Nipáta (London: Published for the Páli Text Society by Luzac & Company, LTD., 1965), p. 62.

applied to any just society. There is an egalitarian nature in confession: from head to bottom or from the Sanghathera to navaka, bhikkhu must follow the confession in the same way. Any member who has committed āpatti confesses it. This is done in the spirit of self-conscious moral purification and the harmony of the Sangha. In the event the Sangha wishes to amend or abolish khuddānukhuddakāni sikkhāpadāni rules the Buddha allowed it to do so.

To avoid a schism, the Buddha visited troubled parties individually. He put pressure on the accused to confess the offence out of faith to other monks. He put pressure on the accuser by telling him that it was not useful, to excommunicate a monk on every occasion. When the Buddha met with both parties together, he preached to them on the dangers of a schism. He spoke on the advantages of concord (sāmaggi). He would try to harmoniously unite them. This is how the schism was healed without causing any violent destruction, or threatening the life of either party.

The majority's opinion is used to satisfy any decision within the Sangha. For purposes of building a new monastery, meting out sanghādisesa punishment, accepting new candidates, re-instating sinners, or selecting monastery sites, the entire Sangha assembles to discuss the matter. A vote is taken with the majority ruling on any action as every member has an equal right to speak out and vote, the majority's view is approved.

The Sangha has, since the time of the Buddha to the present day, been one of the most ideal models of a democratic and social institution in the world. Thus, the Sangha itself must continue to be united and well disciplined. It must be an established foundation for religious social services. Though the prime role of the Sangha is to seek spiritual liberation, it can also instruct, advise, and mobilize people for individual and communal development.

The Sangha has always been in the position of providing moral instruction and counselling with regard to the benefits derived from the harmonious concord of society. The Sangha can also be regarded as a social institution and its values can be approved for the development of a social regime to motivate people to get support for the achievement of political goals. As a democratic ruler under constitutional law impresses the public, so the Sangha, controlled by the disciplinary rules of the vinaya constitution, impresses and influences millions of people with its teachings and practices.

The Sangha is known as a peerless field of merits (puññakkhettaṁ anuttaraṁ). With tremendous faith, people sow their seeds of meritorious deeds by acting generously towards it. They hope to reap a good harvest of merits in the future. People come to monks for advice concerning various things in day to day life. They take the monks' advice as their sole guide. For this reason monks can effectively interfere in any critical situation and secure it from a possible dispute or disaster.

The Sangha has accumulated a tremendous amount of trust through its non-harmful and altruistic ethical practice. Its detached and impartial judgment receives attention from various levels of social and political life. Thus, the Sangha is the central force in various areas of the Buddhist societies world wide. Rich or poor, man or woman, laborer or businessman, teacher or politician, all approach the Sangha. The Sangha is practically one of the oldest continuous democratic societies in the world.

The Sangha members are advised to discuss their daily affairs, observances, the practices of morality, development of meditation, and the teachings of the Buddha. Throughout the Vinaya texts, the Buddha has exhorted his disciples to assemble, discuss and solve problems or decide matters according to the majority's viewpoint.

From the democratic nature of its functioning, its equal consideration of leaders and members, as well as people of all classes and conditions, its strict, clear, yet flexible rules and laws, its emphasis on individual moral development and wisdom, its reliance on its numbers for correction and moral administration, and its harmonious interaction with kings and general public alike, the Sangha proves itself to be an ideal model for modern society.

APPENDIX

The original canonical texts of Theravāda Buddhism comprise the Tipiṭaka, the unsophisticated and straightforward teachings of the Buddha. These texts are fundamental to understanding Buddhist ethics. The Tipiṭaka is divided into three distinct teachings, namely: the Vinaya-Pitaka, the Sutta-Piṭaka and the Abhidhamma-Pitaka. Of these, the Vinaya-Pitaka, which contains the moral codes for the Sangha, or community of monks, has 5 sections: The Mahávagga, The Cullavagga, The Párájiká, The Pácittiya[1] and The Parivára.

The Mahávagga, the first section of the vinaya, contains a narrative of the earliest events of Theravāda Buddhism. The authentic life story of the Buddha is found in this book. It contains accounts of his practice of asceticism, discusses his enlightenment, has the earliest accounts of his fundamental teachings; and also speaks about the establishment of the Sangha. This book, which is the greater collection of themes (mahákhandaka), deals with some of the Buddha's lessons on the duties of preceptor to pupil, and of companion monks towards one another. It also considers the observance of moral practice (uposatha) and examines the commencement and conclusion of the rains retreat ceremony (vassúpanáyika). In addition, it explains the necessary steps that take place during an invitation for moral clarification and admonition (paváraná). It even touches on the use and purpose of the saffron robe (kathina cïvara) which all monks wear.

The second section of the vinaya is the Cullavagga, the lesser collection of the rules. It consists primarily of the description of the rules and regulations that affect the practical operation of the Sangha. The procedure for the training of monks and nuns (bhikkhunï), the formal acts of probation or punishment for members who commit Sanghádisesa, and the guidelines for settling problems within the Sangha are set forth here. The use and purpose of lodgings is also discussed in this section.

---

[1]The Párájiká and The Pácittiya are also classified as The Suttavibhanga (First Part) and The Suttavibhanga (Second Part) respectively. See Hermann Oldenberg, ed., The Vinaya Piṭakaṁ, Vol. III & IV. (London: Published for the Páli Text Society by Luzac & Company, LTD., 1964).

Unlike The Cullavagga, which sets forth rules, the Párájiká is a systematic analysis of the major and minor disciplinary rules of the Sangha. It contains a detailed description of a defeat (párájiká) (a transgression of the rules for which a monk can be expelled from the Sangha). It explains when a formal meeting of the Sangha (sanghádisesa) is necessary, and has "undetermined matters" (violations for which there are not specific rules) (aniyata). It also analyzes the procedure for forfeiture (nissaggiya). This is the core of the Pátimokkha (compendium of monastic rules or reduced version of moral codes).

Rules of expiation (pácittiya), offenses to be confessed (pátidesaniya), methods of moral training (sekhiyá), analysis of nuns' rules (bhikkhunïvibhanga), and settlement of legal questions (adhikarana-samatha) are contained detailed in the Pácittiya, the fourth division of the vinaya.

The Parivára is the last volume of the Vinaya texts. It is a commentary on all the vinaya rules. It includes all materials related to the vinaya and is the supporting material of The Suttavibhangas. It also contains an analysis of a monk's life (bhikkhuvibhanga), the nuns' analysis (same as monks') (bhikkhunïvibhanga), a summary of the origins of rules (samutthánasïsasankhepa), a portion on criticizing or reproving of any monk whose conduct is not proper (chodanákandaṁ), and a collection of stanzas or poems (gáthásaṁganikaṁ). Further, it has a synopsis of legal questions, and concerns itself with the general decision making in the Sangha.

The Vinaya texts have traditional commentaries by Buddhaghosa, a very well known monk who lived about A.D. 300, known as Samantapásádiká. These are a sophisticated interpretation of the texts. The Samantapásádiká analytically and exhaustively deals with the vinaya rules and the major external history of the Buddha. Detailed explanations as to why the Buddha laid down a particular rule are given in addition to the who, what, and where of the rule established. The majority of Buddhist scholars accepts Buddhaghosa's commentaries as traditional. They are still in the old style. That is, they do not show a distinct table of contents except in the last volume, which is the book of indices. Although some of the major subject headings are listed at the top of the stories, most subject matters are mentioned at each conclusion of the story.

Besides the Vinaya texts and commentaries, there are also later scholarly works on these volumes. For example, Somdet Phra Maha Samana Chao Krom

Phraya Vajirañánavarorasa (a prince who became monk and founded Dhammayutta-Nikáya sect about 200 years ago in Thailand) did remarkable work on the Vinaya texts and Commentaries about 200 years ago. He added some of his own experiences and observations to them in his work, known as The Entrance to the Vinaya (Vinayamukha) Vol. I-III. He tried to honestly represent the traditional practices of the Theraváda vinaya rules. Unlike the original texts, his modernization excludes repetition of the stories. He is occasionally critical of the commentarial tradition. However, considering the importance of the authenticity of the vinaya rules, he appeals to vinaya experts to decide critical points which he found uncertain.

The Sutta-Piṭaka is the largest section of the Tipiṭaka. Its principal theme is the discovery of the good law (dhamma) which leads to the final goal of Buddhist practice. That goal is to attain the highest realization of life and absolute mental peace or nibbána. The "summum bonum" of Buddhist practice, it is described as a release from all forms of greed (lobha), hatred (dosa), and delusion (moha). Like the vinaya, the Sutta-Piṭaka is divided into five divisions which are The Dïgha-Nikáya, The Majjhima-Nikáya, The Samyutta-Nikáya, The Anguttara-Nikáya and The Khuddaka-Nikáya. These texts are not, in general, arranged in accordance with their subject matter. Rather they are grouped simply according to their length and nature. The collection of long dialogues, for example, is the section called The Dïgha-Nikáya, while the ones of medium length are known as The Majjhima-Nikáya.

Other various teachings joined together are called The Samyutta-Nikáya, the third section. It contains many groups of Suttas or dialogues. These are divided into various categories according to their themes. The Samyutta contains kindred sayings with verses (sagáthá-vagga), prologues (nidána-vagga), and the subtitles (khandha-vagga). It has a section on the sphere of senses (saláyatana-vagga), and also another called the great sections (mahávagga). B a s i c a l l y , T h e Samyutta-Nikáya contains kindred sayings on various areas of teachings.

The fourth section of the Sutta-Piṭaka is The Anguttara-Nikáya, the gradual teachings or the group of numbered Suttas. It is organized in terms of numerical lists which reflect as, the number of items in each dialogue, the group of ones, twos, threes and so on until the group of elevens (ekaka-nipáta, duka-nipáta, tika-nipáta,... ekádasaka-nipáta).

99

The collection called the small or minor verses is The Khuddaka-Nikáya, the last section of the Sutta-Pitaka. It contains miscellaneous texts. The 15 books in it are: The Khuddakapátha (stories and stanzas), The Dhammapada (short poems), The Udána (exclamations of the Buddha), The Itivuttaka (ethical stories), The Sutta-Nipáta (short verses), The Vimánavatthu (parables), The Petavatthu (parables about spirits of deceased people), The Theragáthá (Elders' sayings), The Therïgáthá (Senior nuns' sayings), The Játaka (stories of the past life of the Buddha), The Niddesa (explanations of the origins if Buddhism), The Patisambhidámagga (stories), The Apadána (stories), The Buddhavamsa (lineage or heritage of Buddhas) and The Cariyápitaka [practice of perfection (páramitá) leading to Buddhahood].

The third and final division of the Tipitaka, the Abhidhamma-Pitaka, is classified into the following divisions: The Dhammasanganï, The Vibhanga, The Dhátukathá, The Puggalapaññatti, The Kathávatthu, The Yamaka, and The Patthána. These texts are mainly devoted to the analysis of consciousness (citta), concomitant mental states (cetasika), form-matter (rúpa) and nibbána (nirvána).

The Abhidhamma-Pitaka is the second largest section of the Tipitaka. Its methodology and style of language show that the Abhidhamma Pitaka was not preached at the same period of time as the Sutta-Pitaka and the Vinaya-Pitaka. The Sutta-Pitaka is in the colloquial language of the day. Almost every Sutta directly addresses an individual, group, or problem as the main cause for the dialogue. Most of the Suttas start with the words, "Evaṁ me sutaṁ" ("thus have I heard..."). From this, one can clearly perceive that Suttas were reported to somebody or to a group (i.e, the First Buddhist Council). In contrast, the Abhidhamma does not address an individual person or persons; neither does it examine specific problems but deals with more general or universal themes. It does not begin with "Evaṁ me sutaṁ"; rather, it is a general statement about universality, phenomena, and nibbána. Theraváda tradition holds that the entire Abhidhamma was so special that it was directly taught by the Buddha to his mother in Tusita heaven. The Abhidhamma's content, as well as its style of language, is very different from that of the Suttas.

It is interesting to note that the two larger Pitakas are devoted mainly to the work of dhamma (good law). Only the first Pitaka deals with vinaya rules (i.e., rules of conduct).

The Sutta-Pitaka's discussions of various ethical rules provide much information on the standards of ethical behavior. Morality (sïla), concentration (samádhi), and insight (paññá) are the fundamental stages of Buddhist practice. Thus, many people incorrectly assume that Theravāda Buddhism is other-worldly and that although the Tipiṭaka texts deal extensively with personal ethics, they contain no political or social principles. Perhaps the origin of this misconception may be found in the fact that the inquiry into societal matters was and is known among Buddhist monks by the derogatory term "animal-like knowledge (tiracchánavijjá)"[2]. For various reasons, these studies are regarded as unimportant in many parts of the Theravāda Buddhist world.

A similar view of the Tipiṭaka texts seems to be held by modern scholars who have addressed the problem of Buddhist ethics. Winston L. King, in his book, In the Hope of Nibbána: the Ethics of Theravāda Buddhism (1964), holds moral discipline as the central concern of Buddhism in people's lives. "What is the relationship of ethics to the total structure of Buddhist doctrine and practice ...?" This is one of the key questions in the book, but King fails to recognize the importance of social theory.

In the Ethics of Buddhism (1926) by S. Tachibana states that morality was the wisdom of Buddhism. His main objective in the book is to prove that in its origin Buddhism is a religion of moral nature but he ignores the social theory in Buddhism.

Siddhi Butr-Indr says that morality obtains a predominant position in social philosophy. He gives some partial recognition to this in his book, The Social Philosophy of Buddhism (1973); however, he, too, misses the central idea of social theory which exists within the Vinaya texts.

Religion and Legitimation of Power in Thailand, Laos, and Burma (1978), edited by Bardwell L. Smith, attempts to judge new ways of interpreting the ongoing relationship between idealogies and social practices dominating the society. Religion and Legitimation of Power in Sri Lanka (1978), edited by Bardwell L.

---

[2]M. Leon Feer, ed., Samyutta-Nikáya, Part III (London: Published for The Páli Text Society by Messrs. Luzac & Company, LTD., 1960), p. 239.

Smith, examines the relationship of religion to the social order in different contexts. But neither of these books deals with the original Buddhist texts.

Walpola Rahula's The Heritage of the Bhikkhu and Somboon Suksamran's Political Buddhism in Southeast Asia (1976) have given some critical thought to the existence of social theory, disguised within the realm of religious concepts (practices). These authors reflect only the contemporary Buddhist societies of Sri Lanka and Thailand respectively and do not deal with the Páli Vinaya texts.

BIBLIOGRAPHY

Primary Sources

Andersen, Dines and Smith, Helmer, eds. Sutta-Nipáta. New Edition. London: Published for the Páli Text Society by Luzac & Company, LTD., 1965.

The Book of the Discipline (Cullavagga). Volume V. Translated by I . B . Horner. London: Luzac & Company LTD., 1952.

The Book of the Discipline (Mahávagga). Volume IV. Translated by I . B . Horner. London: Luzac & Company, LTD., 1962.

The Book of the Discipline (Pácittiya). Volume II. Translated by I.B. Horner. London: Published for the Páli Text Society by Luzac & Company LTD., 1957.

The Book of the Discipline (Párájiká). Volume I. Translated by I.B. Horner. Published for the Páli Text Society by Luzac & Company LTD., London, 1949.

The Book of the Discipline (Vinaya-Piṭaka) (Parivára). Vol. VI. Translated by I.B. Horner. London: Published for the Páli Text Society by Luzac & Company, LTD., 1966.

The Book of the Discipline (Vinaya-Pitaka) (The Mahávagga). Vol. IV. Translated by I.B. Horner. London: Published for the Páli Text Society by Luzac & Company, LTD., 1951.

The Book of the Discipline (Vinaya-Pitaka). Vol. I. Translated by I.B. Horner. London: Published for the Páli Text Society by Luzac & Company, LTD., 1949.

The Book of the Gradual Sayings (Anguttara-Nikáya). Vol. I. Translated by F.L. Woodward. London: Published for the Páli Text Society by Luzac & Company, LTD., 1970.

The Book of the Gradual Sayings (Anguttara-Nikáya). Vol. I. Translated by F.L. Woodward. London: Published for the Páli Text Society by Luzac & Company, LTD., 1960.

The Book of the Gradual Sayings (Anguttara-Nikáya). Vol. I. Translated by F.L. Woodward. London: Published for the Páli Text Society by the Oxford University Press, 1932.

The Book of the Gradual Sayings (Anguttara-Nikáya). Vol. II. Translated by F.L. Woodward. London: Published for the Páli Text Society by Luzac & Company, LTD., 1962.

The Book of the Gradual Sayings (Anguttara-Nikáya). Vol. II. Translated by F.L. Woodward. London: Published by the Páli Text Society, 1973.

The Book of the Gradual Sayings (Anguttara-Nikáya). Vol. III. Translated by E.M. Hare. London: Published for the Páli Text Society by Luzac & Company, LTD., 1961.

The Book of the Gradual Sayings (Anguttara-Nikáya). Vol. III. Translated by E.M. Hare. London: Published for the Páli Text Society by the Oxford University Press, 1934.

The Book of the Gradual Sayings (Anguttara-Nikáya). Vol. IV. Translated by E.M. Hare. London: Published for the Páli Text Society by Luzac & Company, LTD., 1965.

The Book of the Gradual Sayings (Anguttara-Nikáya). Vol. V. Translated by F.L. Woodward. London: Published for the Páli Text Society by Luzac & Company, LTD., 1972.

The Book of the Gradual Sayings (Anguttara-Nikáya). Vol. V. Translated by F.L. Woodward. London: Published for the Páli Text Society by Luzac & Company, LTD., 1961.

The Book of the Gradual Sayings (Anguttara-Nikáya). Vol. V. Translated by F.L. Woodward. London: Published for the Páli text Society by the Oxford University Press, 1936.

The Book of the Kindred Sayings (Samyutta-Nikáya). Part I. Translated by Rhys
    Davids. London: Published for the Páli Text Society by Luzac & Company,
    LTD., 1950.

The Book of the Kindred Sayings (Samyutta-Nikáya). Part II. Translated by Rhys
    Davids. London: Published for the Páli Text Society by Luzac & Company,
    LTD., 1952.

The Book of the Kindred Sayings (Sanyutta-Nikáya). Part III. Translated by F.L.
    Woodward. London: Published for the Páli Text Society by Luzac &
    Company, LTD., 1954.

The Book of the Kindred Sayings (Sanyutta-Nikáya). Part IV. Translated by F.L.
    Woodward. London: Published for the Páli Text Society by Luzac &
    Company, LTD., 1956.

The Book of the Kindred Sayings (Sanyutta-Nikáya). Part V. Translated by F.L.
    Woodward. London: Published for the Páli Text Society by Luzac &
    Company, LTD., 1956.

Carpenter, J. Estlin, ed. The Dïgha-Nikáya. Vol. III. London: Published for the
    Páli Text Society by Henry Frowde, Oxford University Press Warehouse,
    1911.

Carpenter, J. Estlin, ed. The Dïgha-Nikáya. Vol. III. London: Published for the
    Páli Text Society by Luzac & Company, LTD., 1960.

Chalmers, Lord, ed. Buddha's Teachings (Sutta-Nipáta). Massachusetts: Harvard
    University Press, 1932.

Davids, T.W. Ryhs and Carpenter, J. Estlin, eds. The Dhammapada. English
    translation & notes by. S. Radhakrishnan. Madrass: Published by R. Dayal,
    Oxford University Press, 1980.

Davids, T.W. Rhys and Carpenter, J. Estlin, eds. The Dïgha-Nikáya. Vol. I.
    London: Published by the Páli Text Society, 1975.

Davids, T.W. Rhys and Carpenter, J. Estlin, eds. The Dïgha-Nikáya Vol. II. London: Oxford University Press, 1947.

The Dhammapada. Páli Text and Translation With Stories in Brief   a n d Notes by Narada. Colombo: Vajirarama, 2515/1972.

Dhammapada. Translated by Buddharakkhita. Bangalore: Buddha Vacana Trust, Maha Bodhi Society, 1966.

Dhammapada. Translated by Narada. Vajirarama, Colombo, 2507/1963.

Dialogues of the Buddha (Dïgha-Nikáya). Part I. Translated by T.W. Rhys Davids. London: Luzac & Company, LTD., 1956.

Dialogues of the Buddha (Dïgha-Nikáya). Part I. Translated by T.W. Rhys Davids. London: Published for the Páli Text Society by Luzac & Company, LTD., 1973.

Dialogues of the Buddha (The Dïgha-Nikáya). Part II. Translated by T.W. and C.A.F. Rhys Davids. Published for the Páli Text Society by Luzac & Company, LTD., 1971.

Dialogues of the Buddha (Dïgha-Nikáya). Part II. Translated by T.W. and C.A.F. Rhys Davids. London: Published for the Páli Text Society by Luzac & Company, LTD., 1959.

Dialogues of the Buddha (The Dïgha-Nikáya). Part III. Translated by T.W. and C.A.F. Rhys Davids. London: Published for the Páli Text Society by Luzac & Company, LTD., 1971.

Dialogues of the Buddha (Dïgha-Nikáya). Part III. Translated by T.W. and C.A.F Rhys Davids. London: Published for the Páli Text Society by Luzac Company, LTD., 1965.

Dialogues of the Buddha (Dïgha-Nikáya). Translated by T.W. and C.A.F. Rhys Davids. London: Published for the Páli Text Society by Luzac & Company, LTD., 1971.

The Expositor (Atthasálinï). (Reprint). Vol. I. Translated by Pe Maung Tin. London: the Páli Text Society, 1958.

Feer, M. Leon, ed. The Samyutta-Nikáya of the Sutta-Piṭaka. Part I. London: Published for the Páli Text Society by Luzac & Company, LTD., 1960.

Feer, M. Leon, ed. Samyutta-Nikáya. Part II. London: Published for the Páli Text Society by Luzac & Company, LTD., 1960.

Feer, M. Leon, ed. Samyutta-Nikáya. Part III. London: Published for the Páli Text Society by Luzac & Company, LTD., 1960.

Feer, M. Leon, ed. The Samyutta-Nikáya. Part IV. London: Published for the Páli Text Society by Luzac & Company, LTD., 1960.

Feer, M. Leon, ed. Samyutta-Nikáya. Part V. London: Published for the Páli Text Society by Luzac & Company, LTD., 1960.

Hardy, E., ed. The Anguttara-Nikáya. Part III. London: Published for the Páli Text Society by Luzac & Company, LTD., 1958.

Hardy, E., ed. The Anguttara-Nikáya. Vol. IV. London: Published for the Páli Text Society by Luzac & Company, LTD., 1958.

Hardy, E., ed. The Anguttara-Nikáya. Vol. V. London: Published for the Páli Text Society by Luzac & Company, LTD., 1958.

Kashyap, J., ed. The Anguttara Nikáya. Chakkanipáta, Sattakanipáta & Atthakanipáta. Bihar: Páli Publication Board, (Bihar Government), B.E. 2504/1960.

Kashyap, J., ed. The Patthána. Part I. Bihar: Páli Publication Board, (Bihar Government), B.E. 2505/1961.

Kashyap, J., ed. The Patthána. Part IV. Bihar: Páli Publication Board, (Bihar Government), B.E. 2505/1961.

Kashyap, J., ed. The Vibhanga. Bihar: Páli Publication Board, (Bihar Government), B.E. 2504/1960.

The Middle Length Sayings (Majjhima-Nikáya). VoLume I. Translated by I.B. Horner. London: Published for the Páli Text Society by Luzac & Company, LTD., 1967.

The Middle Length Sayings (Majjhima-Nikáya). Vol. I. Translated by I.B. Horner. London: Published for the Páli Text Society by Luzac & Company, LTD., 1954.

The Middle Length Sayings (Majjhima-Nikáya). Vol. II. Translated by I.B. Horner. London: Published for the Páli Text Society by Luzac & Company, LTD., 1970.

The Middle Length Sayings (Majjhima-Nikáya). Vol. II. Translated by I.B. Horner. London: Published for the Páli Text Society by Luzac & Company, LTD., 1957.

The Middle Length Sayings (Majjhima-Nikáya). Vol. III. Translated by I.B. Horner. London: Published for the Páli Text Society by Luzac & Company, LTD., 1967.

The Middle Length Sayings (Majjhima-Nikáya). Vol. III. Translated by I.B. Horner. London: Published for the Páli Text Society by Luzac & Company, LTD., 1959.

Morris, Richard, ed. Anguttara-Nikáya. Part I. Second Edition. Revised by A.K. Warder. London: Published for the Páli Text Society by Luzac & Company, LTD., 1961.

Morris, Richard; Landsberg, Georg; and Davids, Rhys, eds. Puggalapaññatti and Atthakathá. London: Published for the Páli Text Society by Luzac & Company, LTD., 1972.

Oldenberg, Hermann, ed. The Vinaya Piṭakaṁ (The Mahávagga). Vol. I. London: Published for the Páli Text Society by Luzac & Company LTD., 1964.

Oldenberg, Hermann, ed. The Vinaya Pitakaṁ (The Cullavagga). Vol. II. London: Published for the Páli Text Society by Luzac & Company, LTD., 1964.

Oldenberg, Hermann, ed. The Vinaya Piṭakaṁ (The Suttavibhanga). Vol. III. London: Published for the Páli Text Society by Luzac & Company, LTD., 1964.

Oldenberg, Hermann, ed. The Vinaya Pitakaṁ (The Suttavibhanga). Vol. IV. London: Published for the Páli Text Society by Luzac & Company, LTD., 1964.

Oldenberg, Hermann, ed. The Vinaya Pitakaṁ (The Parivára). Vol. V. London: Published for the Páli Text Society by Luzac & Company, LTD., 1964.

Smith, Helmer, ed. The Khuddaka-Pátha together with its Commentary Paramatthajotiká. I. London: Published for the Páli Text Society by Luzac & Company, LTD., 1959.

Windisch, Ernst, ed. Iti-Vuttaka. Published for the Páli Text Society by Geoffrey Cumberlege, Oxford University Press, 1948.

Woven Cadences of Early Buddhists (Sutta-Nipáta). Translated by E.M. Hare. London: Oxford University Press, 1947.

Commentaries

Buddhaghosa. The Path of Purification (Visuddhimagga). Translated by Bhikkhu Ñánamoli. Ceylon: Published by R. Semage, Colombo, 1956.

Buddhaghosa. The Path of Purification (Visuddhimagga). Translated by Bhikkhu Nyanamoli. Second Edition. Colombo: Published by A Semage, 1964.

Buddhaghosa. The Path of Purification (Visudhimagga). Vol. I. Translated by Bhikkhu Nyanamoli. California: Shambhala Publication, Inc., 1976.

Buddhist Legends (The Dhammapada Commentary). Part I. Translated by Eugene Watson Burlingame. London: Published for the Páli Text Society by Luzac & Company, LTD., 1969.

Buddhist Legends (The Dhammapada Commentary). Part 2. Translated by Eugene Watson Burlingame. London: Published for the Páli Text Society by Luzac & Company, LTD., 1969.

Buddhist Legends (The Dhammapada Commentary). Part 3. Translated by Eugene Watson Burlingame. London: Published for the Páli Text Society by Luzac & Company, LTD., 1969.

Davids, T.W. Rhys and Carpenter, J. Estlin, eds. The Sumangala-Vilásinï, Buddhaghosa's Commentary on the Dïgha-Nikáya. Part I. Second Edition. London: Published for the Páli Text Society by Luzac & Company, LTD., 1968.

Dhammapadatthakathá (The Commentary on the Dhammapada). Vol. I. London: Published for the Páli Text Society by Luzac & Company, LTD., 1970.

Fausboll, V., ed. The Játaka Together with its Commentary being Tales of the Anterior Births of Gotama Buddha. Vol. I. London: Published for the Páli Text Society by Luzac & Company, LTD., 1962.

Fausboll, V., ed. The Játaka Together with its Commentary Being Tales of the Anterior Births of Gotama Buddha. Vol. II. London: Published for the Páli Text Society by Luzac & Company, LTD., 1963.

Fausboll, V., ed. The Játaka Together With Its Commentary.
Vol. III. London: Published for the Páli Text Society by Luzac & Company, LTD., 1963.

The Inception of the Discipline and the Vinaya Nidána.
Translated and edited by N.A. Jayawickrama. London: Luzac & Company, LTD., 1962.

The Játaka or Stories of the Buddha's Former Births. Vol. II. Translated by W.H.D. Rouse. London: Published for the Páli Text Society by Luzac & Company, LTD., 1957.

The Játaka or Stories of the Buddha's Former Births. Vol. III. Translated by H.T. Francis and R.A. Neil. London: Published for the Páli Text Society by Luzac & Company, LTD., 1957.

The Játaka or Stories of the Buddha's Former Births. Vol. IV. Translated by W.H.D. Rouse. London: Published for the Páli Text Society by Luzac & Company, LTD., 1973.

The Játaka or Stories of the Buddha's Former Births. Vol. V. Translated by H.T. Francis. London: Published by the Páli Text Society, 1973.

Kopp, Hermann, compiled. Samantapásádiká Buddhaghosa's Commentary on the Vinaya Pitaka. Vol. VIII. London: Published by the Páli Text Society, LTD., 1977.

The Mahávastu. Volume I. Translated from the Buddhist Sanskrit by J.J. Jones. London: Luzac & Company, LTD., 1949.

Norman, H.C., ed. Dhammapadatthakathá. Vol. I. London: Published for the Páli Text Society by Luzac & Company, LTD., 1970.

Norman, H.C. ed. The Commentary on the Dhammapada. Vol. I. London: Published for the Páli Text Society by Luzac & Company, LTD., 1970.

Silva, Lily De, ed. Dïghanikáya Atthakathátïká Linatthavannaná. Vol. II. London: Published for the Páli Text Society by Luzac & Company, LTD., 1970.

The Sumangala-Vilásinï, Buddhaghosa's Commentary on the Dïgha Nikáya. Part I. London: Published for the Páli Text Society by Luzac & Company, LTD., 1968.

Takakusu, J. and M. Nagai, eds. Samantapásádiká Buddhaghosa's Commentary on the Vinaya Pitaka. Vol. I. London: Published by the Páli Text Society, 1975.

Takakusu, J. and M. Nagai, eds. Samantapásádiká Buddhaghosa's Commentary on the Vinaya Pitaka. Vol. II. London: Published for the Páli Text Society by Luzac & Company, LTD., 1969.

Takakusu, J. and M. Nagai, eds. Samanta-Pásádiká Buddhaghosa's Commentary on the Vinaya Pitaka. Vol. III. London: Published for the Páli Text Society by Luzac & Company, LTD., 1968.

Takakusu, J. and Makato Nagai, eds. Samantapásádiká Buddhaghosa's Commentary on the Vinaya Pitaka. Vol. IV. London: Published for the Páli Text Society by Luzac & Company, LTD., 1967.

Takakusu, J. and M. Nagai, eds. Samantapásádiká Buddhaghosa's Commentary on the Vinaya Pitaka. Vol. V. London: Published for the Páli Text Society by Luzac & Company, LTD., 1966.

Takakusu, J. and M. Nagai, eds. Samantapásádiká Buddhaghosa's Commentary on the Vinaya Pitaka. Vol. VI. London: Published for the Páli Text Society by Luzac & Company, LTD., 1947.

Takakusu, J. and M. Nagai, eds. Samantapásádiká Buddhaghosa's Commentary on the Vinaya Pitaka. Vol. VII. London: Published for the Páli Text Society by Luzac & Company, LTD., 1947.

Vajirañána, ed. Mangalatthadïpanï. Second Edition by Nanavara thera Buddhaghosácáriya. First Volume. Siam: Published by Mahámakutarájavidyálaya, B.E. 2517.

Warren, Henry Clarke, ed. Visuddhimagga of Buddhaghosácáriya. Revised by Dharmananda Kosambi. Cambridge: Harvard University Press, 1950.

Secondary Sources

Amritananda. <u>Buddhakálïn Mahiláharú</u>. Part I. (Nepali Language).
Kathmandu: Published by Ananda Kuti Vihar Trust, 1973.

Amritananda. <u>Buddhakálïna Rájaparivára</u>. Volume I. (Nepali Language).
Kathmandu: Published by Anandakuti Vihara Guthi, B.E. 2515.

Barua, Rabindra. <u>The Theraváda Sangha</u>. Published by M.R. Tarafdar. The
Asiatic Society of Bangladesh, 1978.

Buddhaghosha. <u>Paritrána</u> With Meaning and Introduction. (Devanágarï script).
Nepal: Subhash Printing Press, Yala, B.E. 2527/1983.

<u>Buddhist Scriptures</u>. Selected and translated by Edward Conze. Maryland: Penguin
Books, 1969.

Butr-Indr, Siddhi. <u>The Social Philosophy of Buddhism</u>. Bangkok: Published by
Mahamakut Buddhist University, 1979.

Davids, T.W. and Stede, William, eds. <u>Páli English Dictionary</u>. London: Published
by the Páli Text Society, 1979.

Dutta, Sukumar. <u>Buddhist Monks and Monasteries of India</u>. London: Printed in
Great Britain by C. Tinling & Co. LTD., 1962.

Fowler, H.W. and Fowler, F.G. eds. <u>The Concise Oxford Dictionary   o   f
Current English</u>. Fifthy Edition. London: Oxford University Press, 1964.

Gombrich, Richard F. <u>Precept and Practice</u>. Oxford University Press, 1971.

<u>Itten Shikai Kaiki Myoho</u>. Tokyo: Published by Japan-Bharat Sarvodaya Mitra
Sangha, 1985.

James, Gene G. ed. <u>The Family and the Unification Church</u>. New York:
Unification Theological Seminary, Barrytown, 1983.

113

K., Sri Dhammananda. What Buddhists Believe. Kuala Lumpur: Published by the Buddhist Missionary Society, 1982.

King, Winston L. In the Hope of Nibbana The Ethics of Theravāda Buddhism. Illinois: The Open Court Publishing Company, 1964.

Lavine, T.Z. From Socrates to Sartre: the Philosophic Quest. New York: Bantam Books, Inc., 1984.

Malalasekera, G.P. Dictionary of the Páli Proper Names. Vol. I & II. London: Published for the Páli Text Society by Luzac & Company, LTD., 1960.

Milinda-Prashna. (Hindi Language). Translated by Jagadisha Kashyapa. Culcatta: Dharmodaya Sabha, B.E. 2495/1957.

Narada, ed. & tr. A Manual of Abhidhamma Being Abhidhammattha Sangaha of Bhadanta Anuruddhácáriya. Colombo: Buddhist Publication Society, 1968.

Na-Rangsi, Sunthorn. The Buddhist Concepts of Karma and Rebirth. Bangkok: Mahámakut Rájavidyálaya Press, 1976/2519.

Narasabho, Singhathon. Buddhism a Guide to a Happy Life. Bangkok: Maháchulongkornrájavidyálaya, 1971.

Narasu, P. Lakshmi. What is Buddhism. Third Edition. Calcutta: Published by Davapriya Valisinha, Mahabodhi Society of India, 1964.

Pragyananda and Dharmaloka, eds. Paritta Sutta. (Devanágari script) Nepal: Subhash Printing Press, Lalitpur, B.E. 2517.

The Questions of King Milinda. Part I. Translated from the Páli by T.W. Rhys Davids. New York: Dover Publications, Inc., 1963.

Rahula, Walpola. The Heritage of the Bhikkhu. New York: Grove Press, Inc., 1974.

Rahula, Walpola. What the Buddha Taught. New York: Grove Press, Inc., 1959.

114

Sásanasobhana, ed. <u>Svadmantplae</u>. Thai Character Páli Language. 8th Print. Bangkok: Mahámakutarájavidyálaya Press, 2522.

Smith, Donold Eugene. <u>Religion and Politics in Burma</u>. New Jersey: Princeton University Press, 1965.

Spiro, Melford E. <u>Buddhism and Society</u>. California: University of California Press, 1982.

Stein, Jess, ed. <u>The Random House Dictionary</u>. New York: Ballantine Books, 1980.

Suksamran, Somboon. <u>Political Buddhism in Southeast Aisa</u>. New York: St. Martin's Press, 1977.

Suzuki, Daisetz Teitaro. <u>Outlines of Maháyána Buddhism</u>. New York: Schocken Books, 1963.

Tachibana, S. <u>The Ethics of Buddhism</u>. Reprint. London: Published by Curzon Press Ltd., Barnes & Noble Books, 1981.

Turabian, Kate L. <u>A Manual for Writers of Term Papers, Theses, and Dissertations</u>. Fourth Edition. Chicago: The University of Chicago, 1973.

Vajirañána, M. <u>Life of a Lay Buddhist</u>. Kuala Lumpur: Published by the Buddhist Missionary Society, 1981.

Vajirañánavarorasa, ed. <u>Dhamma Vibhaga Numerical Sayings of Dhamma</u>. (With explanation and notes) Part Two. Bangkok: Mahámakut Rájavidyálaya Press, 2518/1975.

Vajirañánavarorasa. <u>The Entrance to the Vinaya</u> (<u>Vinayamukha</u>). Vol. I. Bangkok: Mahámakutarájavidyálaya, 2512/1969.

Vajirañánavarorasa. <u>The Entrance to the Vinaya Vinayamukha</u>, Vol. I. Bangkok: Mahámakut Rájavidyálaya Press, 2526/1983.

Vajirañánavarorasa. The Entrance to the Vinaya Vinayamukha. Vol. III. Bangkok: Mahámakut Rájavidyálaya Press, 2526/1983.

Vajirañánavarorasa, ed. Navakováda. Instruction for Newly-Ordained Bhikkhus and Sámaneras. Bangkok: Mahámakutarájavidyálaya, Mahámakut Buddhist University, 2514/1971.

INDEX

BIOGRAPHICAL SKETCH

The Reverend Sunanda Putuwar, ordained Buddhist Priest, the middle son of Mr. Kajibahadura and Mrs. Dirghamaya Putuwar, Banepa, Nepal, received a doctoral degree in Philosophy (1988) from The American University's College of Arts and Sciences.

A 1978 graduate of Mahamakut Buddhist University in Bangkok, Thailand, Putuwar also holds a Master of Arts degree (1981) from Banaras Hindu University, India, and a Master of Theological Studies degree (1984) from Harvard Divinity School.

He has authored books, Karma: (in Newari) (B.E. 2525), Shishtácára (Social etiquette, in Newari) (B.E. 2525), and numerous articles on Buddhist subjects. He is a teacher and frequently interprets Buddhism to a wide variety of audiences.